The Alchemy of Performance Anxiety

Transformation for Artists

Clare Hogan

First published in 2018 by
Free Association Books

A CIP Catalogue of this book is available from the British Library

ISBN: 978-1-91138-319-2

Typeset by
Typo•glyphix
www.typoglyphix.co.uk

Cover design by
Sarah Smith Design

Printed and bound in England

Contents

Contents

Foreword

The focus of this book is on the application of psychological alchemical practice to address, explore and examine the nature and cause of anxiety in order to tackle and overcome it. The first half of the book identifies the issues to be considered and the second half explains and illustrates the alchemical practices with which to approach them. One of the aims is to demonstrate the links between seemingly different ideologies, the concept of spiritual science (currently popular with neuroscientists in particular) and also the 'science of art' which lies at the heart of both the book and of alchemy.

Spiritual science may be 'on trend' but it isn't new. Alchemy has ceased to be quite so esoteric since J.K. Rowling brought it into mainstream culture via a powerful adolescent vehicle. However, while the word alchemy might occupy more frequent use in daily speech, it rarely refers to the complexity of the alchemical process nor to the significance of its ancient spiritual and scientific practice. It is both a science and an art emanating from spirituality (not religion) and it has never been more timely to illustrate the reality that scientific, artistic and spiritual understanding, together with practical application, has the capacity to eliminate anxiety and gain personal control, liberation and fulfilment.

The book is designed as a personal development book rather than a scholarly work and, although it is relevant to all ages (depending on timing), it was written with eighteen to thirty year olds as the main inspiration and audience, both through apparent and ever increasing necessity.

The intention is for this book to be used rather than studied chronologically and, just as there are many observations within it of the cyclic nature of all life, so too is there a potentially cyclic element contained within the text depending on its use. For example, if the chapter on silence feels more resonant initially then there's no need to wade through seven chapters in order to reach it; they will come around as and when they are needed. While it can be read from cover to cover, from which the reader will benefit from developmental thought and investigation, its primary function is its use and accessibility in order to understand that control of one's experience and liberation from anxiety and suffering is not only possible, but within everyone's capacity to achieve – hence its accessible length and language.

Each chapter has the potential for academic exploration and research, which wouldn't be suitable here, but references are provided so readers can do further research should they wish to. It is a source book that can be dipped into anywhere or can launch further investigation into any of the various disciplines and practices covered. Alchemy has the capacity to bind it all together and the alchemy of performance can become a way of life for anyone.

Introduction

This book is about the correspondence between alchemy and metaphysical law with particular reference to the subject of performance. It will focus primarily on musical performance, but can be interpreted and applied with equal validity to any manifestation of performance in its multiple guises in human life. It also addresses the necessity for repetition in all areas of life and, although there is a chapter devoted to this idea, the underlying truth of it permeates the book.

Those who undergo the application of deliberate and concentrated repetition in order to achieve specific outcomes and results realise the absolute and fundamental need for the mind to be reprogrammed, which can be achieved by frequent repetition of specific psychological input. The truths expounded herein apply to every aspect of human existence and the perception of apparently unexplored links together with their application to creative and artistic endeavour are shared and encouraged.

This book, then, is directed at 'performers' – that is to say, everybody, because we are all performers. The difference is simply the level of consciousness at which we engage in it. In the world of music, drama, dance, and public life in general, there is a deliberate decision to behave in a fashion that is consciously studied to display an acquired skill. The words 'deliberate' and 'conscious' define the difference between this type of performance and that which is engaged in by all people by default: children, adults, adolescents (particularly).

To perform is to act in fulfilment of function. Who doesn't do that? Who doesn't adapt their behaviour according to their environment? One only has to consider behaviour within the confines of a car in contrast to, say, a theatre or a church.

The principle tenet of this book is that we are responsible for our experience and if that is anything other than we would wish, only we as individuals have the capacity to improve it in any lasting and meaningful way. We do this with our thoughts and our imagination. As with the acquisition of any skill, it requires practice and repetition – constant repetition in order to change our minds. Our minds are changeable, but to achieve that requires deliberate, repetitive, and playful practice. And so, we will begin with play.

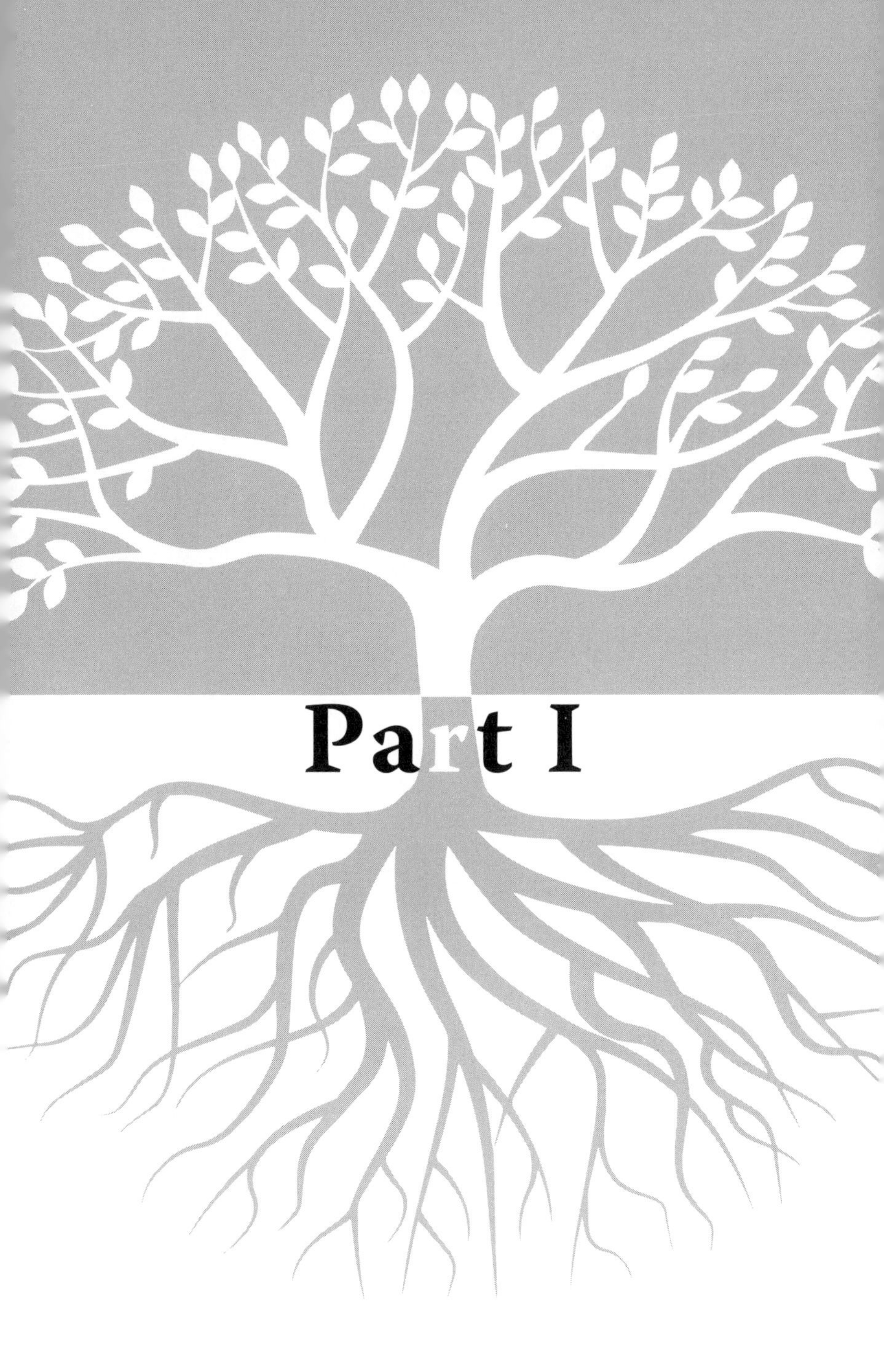

Part I

I. Play and Practice

Efficiency and Fun

Everything associated with the notion of play is attractive. It promotes ideas of leisure, freedom, imagination, and release. We imagine this to be our ideal state of being and feel the need to deserve this condition, this state of sheer enjoyment. Consider the verb, 'deserve'. It has many connotations suggesting good behaviour and reward, which means that we don't feel it to be our natural right and expectation to experience joy, enthusiasm, and exhilaration. These are considered to be earned privileges, occasional rather than habitual.

We also associate play with children. We were children. The unrestricted imagination is the most creative tool we possess, and it isn't acquired – it is lost. As children, our imagination is most of what we are; we haven't lived long enough to be constrained by 'reality', nor have we learned how to harness our limitless visions into the life experiences that we choose. (Most adults haven't either.) Small children are uninhibited which enables them to freely roam between their world(s) within and that without and this is how they develop. They are not constrained by the imposition of delayed gratification and learning outcomes or future goals. Of course, inhibition becomes necessary to some degree; there would be social anarchy if we always acted impulsively. But the subtle levels of inhibition and the many roots beneath their acquisition can cause crippling loss of confidence and self-esteem later.

It is an interesting observation that we repeatedly re-fer, re-vise, re-member, re-habilitate, re-activate, and re-peat so much of what we knew from our earliest years of consciousness. The physical, psychological, and emotional freedom and the confidence that should be our natural state is a sad loss at the very least, and one so great that many of us spend years, fortunes, and relationships trying to understand and come to terms with it.

We are designed to play and to have fun. Play means creation and we are all creators, deliberately or otherwise. Because we think, we create, be it good, bad, or neutral. We mostly react to circumstances unconsciously and this emotional spasm is responsible for our experience of the world. We learn best when we are enjoying ourselves for two reasons: first, our *vibrational levels* are high and therefore receptive (explained and explored in chapters III, V and VII), and second, there is little or no resistance. The word play is used in all aspects of producing music: we play an instrument, we play CDs, vinyl, decks. We play at recitals, gigs, concerts, and venues; musical compositions: fugues, symphonies, sonatas. These are just some musical examples of the multiple aspects of our lives that suggest we are mostly enjoying ourselves.

While it may be all play, it certainly isn't all fun. For many it involves struggle, worry, resistance, and confusion. What happens to us from around the age of five that causes such a shift in our attitude to learning? After all, we often have to learn to play. Our education system promotes expectation and measurement from the outset. Young children quickly become aware that they must learn and prove they have learned, and must also fulfil learning outcomes. This constraint affects them years before they have any idea what learning outcomes are and the consequent self-consciousness that develops often results in fear of underachievement and consequent sense of inadequacy. So, the seeds of competition and anxiety are sown and the enjoyment begins to wane.

Prior to this, during the years when children learn more than at any other time in their lives, they are free to enjoy the world; touch it, taste it, smell it, imagine and make-believe it. This is the enjoyable exploration of their inner and outer world, gradually conflating the two at their own pace and need, resulting in intense growth and development through curiosity and exploration. A child's learning strategies don't suddenly alter at the ages of four or five. The demands made of them do, and it isn't only the psychological expansion that can begin to atrophy. Physical poise, natural movement, and grace also become limited and constrained. Imperial College, London, has carried out extensive research on the effects of the drug LSD and discovered that with a dose as small as 75mcg regions of the (healthy adult) brain that were usually segregated began to speak to each other as if the drug reversed the restricted thinking that develops between infancy and adulthood. David Nutt, the former government drugs adviser says,

'This is to neuroscience what the Higgs boson was to particle physics.' (Of which more in chapter VII.) The potential of LSD to cure mental illness and to deepen our understanding of consciousness itself is one of the most exciting developments in all areas of human development, not least because a deeper understanding of its production and application could not only arrest the onset of restricted thinking, but actually liberate us from it altogether.

In his book, *Play Anything,* Ian Bogost explores the fundamental concepts of play and fun, and redefines them:

> 'I will upset the deep and intuitive beliefs you hold about seemingly simple concepts, like play and its supposed result, fun. It's not only that we don't know how to play effectively; it's also that our ordinary sense of the term is wrong. We think that in play, we do what we want, that we release ourselves from external duty and obligation and finally yield to our clearest, innermost desires. We think we know what we want and we believe that we are in control of our fates, but all of these beliefs are mistaken.'

He then explores the premise that our perception of and attitudes towards play are both in need of a seismic shift. 'Play, generalised, is the operation of structures, constrained by limitations.' He discusses at length – an entire chapter in fact – the idea that fun is novelty rather than pleasure.

> '[Fun] demands seeking out novelty within the boundaries of playgrounds. Fun is the cold, indifference of something that just is what it is. Fun is exploration [...] to discover novelty in something familiar.'

He is saying that it is our attitudes that require attention in order to enhance our experience. The subject of attitude is the main focus of the next chapter. Play and fun result from having the capacity to find something new and engaging in the familiar and repetitive events of daily life. For the deliberate adoption of any form of play, practice has to be involved. Efficiency and Fun

Practice is a multi-faceted behaviour that has attracted, and continues to attract, a great deal of attention. When we consider practice we must ask whether or not it is well organised and goal orientated or aimless and haphazard. It is certainly a necessary activity and the primary one for any serious musician – indeed for anyone attempting to develop and acquire a new skill – and no-one has become either accomplished or truly successful without it. The scientific concept of practice is more detailed than our general notion of it. There is both formal and informal practice, but both share the goal of developing complex mental and physical adaptations that will enable long-term skill-building and achievement.

Most of us have an ambivalent attitude towards practice, which shifts and changes according to our levels of desire and optimism. (This will undergo closer examination in the following chapter.) There are different types of practice, many of which are frequently overlooked due to our misguided ideas of what practice entails. The Alexander Technique, meditation, reading a personal development book or concentrated listening are all forms of practice; they assist in developing complex and holistic connections that enable long-term growth. Many of these activities are referred to as 'a' practice, switching from verb to noun. For example, the practices of yoga and meditation.

I. Play and Practice

The love-hate relationship that is often felt towards the subject of practice is caused by the need for self-motivation, often without very much desire. The necessary discipline is what reduces the numbers of successful (even competent) musicians, in that, given the number of children who take up an instrument, remarkably few become any good at it. I suggest one of the reasons for this is that very few teachers study the subject of practice and consequently don't know how to teach it, irrespective of age. In deliberate practice, during which a student is trying to exceed previous limits, full concentration and effort are required. Both of these words nearly always elicit some level of resistance, despite the fact that the activity is voluntary. To practice effectively (and to teach it), one needs a rudimentary knowledge of brain function. Concentration and effort are both extremely demanding and can only be maintained for approximately twenty minutes, because the human concentration span is short. This doesn't mean we can only do any meaningful activity for very short periods of time; it means we can learn to recognise when our focus on any one issue needs shifting. More practice doesn't equal better performance, because the number of hours is irrelevant. The quality of mental effort is what matters, which means that short and efficient practice periods are essential.

The key is to know that nothing we do has to continue for too long. Understanding the broad spectrum of what is meant by practice and learning how to maximise the use of one's brain can be liberating. If a practice room has been booked for two hours, a great deal can be achieved, but certainly not on any single point. Preparation is needed before the two hours so that a practice strategy is ready to go. By dividing up the time, not necessarily into six twenty-minute parts because there could be some rotation, we know that however challenging any part of the session might be, the time spent on it is finite and not dependent on achievement, which means that mental strain should not occur. Two hours of variety lie ahead, rather than of frustration, boredom, and 'hard work'.

The trick is to shift to another aspect of learning when things are going well. This is known as resting at peaks. It has a highly positive effect on the psyche and raises levels of enthusiasm and desire. Also, whatever the attention is shifted to is approached not only with a fully functional brain but also an emotional energy that, when present, enables information to be most rapidly absorbed. In addition, while the next part of the practice is under way, the brain is processing the previous one and the state in which it does this is critical to the outcome. Knowing when to get out of the way and trust the brain is probably one of the most rewarding lessons to learn; we are not fighting our brain with resistance and frustration, but trusting it to sort, file, and cross-reference without interference. Practice must be learned and therefore taught. It should be a holistic behavioural undertaking, which is largely governed by *feeling*. Emotion is far more powerful than thought, and learning to work with the brain rather than arguing with it is an essential component in teaching and executing efficient and enjoyable practice.

We all do this anyway, at times, and choose activities that promote a feeling of selflessness. When we decide to go to the theatre, see a film or read a particular book, it is often because we hope to be so absorbed that we 'lose ourselves', and our preoccupation with ourselves temporarily ceases. We describe this as fun. Why is it fun to lose oneself? It is because we experience effortless concentration which we are able to maintain for much longer than twenty minutes and because the part of the brain that never stops talking, mostly critical, judgemental, repetitive chatter, to some degree becomes quiet. It is a relief rather like having a short holiday from oneself. We don't become mentally dysfunctional – quite the reverse. In Western society it is normal behaviour to invest time and money in often unpredictable events in the hope of experiencing a psychological and emotional shift which is considered to be beneficial. The point here is that this internal shift can be achieved at any time through the practice of meditation which is able to provide the required benefits almost on demand. Very young children can be natural meditators and, as with so many gifts we are born with, we have to learn them all over again decades later.

Recalling Ian Bogost's definition of fun, it is a state of mind over which we have control, and is experienced through, and relies mainly on, attitude and motivation.

II. Attitude and Motivation

Perception and Assumption

Imagine if every day was Friday. Imagine if every Monday was a Bank Holiday. Imagine if the weekend lasted all week. How wonderful life would be for those whose attitude is so affected by habitual reactions to accepted social experience. There are many who loathe Mondays so intensely that Sunday is ruined in anticipation. Conversely, at the other end of the spectrum (the spectrum being four days), Thursday is the new Friday because the anticipation is so great that Friday itself cannot live up to its own reputation arising from our emotional investment.

Imagination creates the world – that's how powerful it is – but most humans don't use it in a deliberate and conscious fashion. It roams aimlessly through an amorphous fog of repetitive and predictable thought patterns, not daring to travel beyond a certain point. To imagine that every day is Friday feels to be preposterous; it *feels* to be impossible to truly imagine – such is the extent of our conditioning.

Monday cannot, of itself, be bleak. Our feelings govern our attitude about Monday, Friday – every day, month, event, indeed every anticipated pattern of reaction that we hang on to, passively or not.

A day of the week cannot be held responsible for anyone's attitude towards it. The imagination is responsible for feeling, reaction and attitude. Everything everywhere begins with and is a result of it – if it can be imagined, it exists. Imagination is a thinking, intelligent substance, infinitely creative and malleable and manifesting constantly. It responds to (takes its orders from) the conscious mind and is utterly obedient to its thoughts and assumptions. Therefore, our thoughts and assumptions create our experience. The most challenging part of this to accept is the responsibility it bestows. Initially, it may sound incredible, then highly improbable, then require proof (of which more later) and then may sound too good to be true.

The truth is not in question, as truth cannot be, but it can be hard to accept that the miserable events of our lives have been attracted and perpetuated by our own states of mind. It usually takes time and mental application to overcome the inevitable resistance, but herein lies liberation – the knowledge (and responsibility) that you are master of your fate. All that is required is mental control over your thoughts, your internal dialogues and your attitude. This is achieved by making conscious use of your imagination.

It is the means by which we can develop the capacity to overcome fear, poverty, illness and anxiety. Of course, we use our imagination anyway, but usually in a passive, chaotic fashion, simply drifting aimlessly through a conglomeration of mostly inattentive, petty dramas, plotting revenge and having arguments which we generally win. It is, almost always, a repetitive, directionless mess.

> *Imagination is the only redemptive power in the universe.*
>
> — Neville Goddard

Man is indispensable for the completion of creation ... he is himself the second creator of the world.

— Carl Jung

'It is like a psychic reality, a subtle body that we tune into when we create. It acts as a bridge between the visible and invisible world.'

– Alice Bailey

How does this affect (musical) performance? How can't it? In any situation in which decisions have to be made about someone else's performance, how much does one rely on standardised test results and how much on a person's motivation and attitude which, in turn, have imagination as their source and inspiration?

Why, for example, does a school, university or other institution call people for interview having received their CV? They need to see, feel and experience their performances as creative human beings. A person's statistical identity is only one small component in ascertaining how potentially successful they might be. The qualities that actually matter most cannot be measured by formal tests and statistics. They can only be measured exercising judgement by an expert drawing on the large unconscious database acquired over many years in order to conclude that the necessary motivation and attitude are present. This is the combination of rational analysis and instinctive judgment, which is another way of describing how two (or more) subconscious minds explore and 'interview' each other while on the surface an entirely different exchange is taking place. This is also why seemingly successful auditions/interviews full of camaraderie and a false sense of friendly security so often result in rejection. The *real* interview occurred at quite a different level.

Music and Motivation

There are multiple sources of motivation in music. We will, predictably, consider them under the categories of intrinsic and extrinsic.

Music is intrinsically motivating and initially we engage in it for its own sake. It is inherently human to be attracted to music, even if only as something to listen to, and this fact is used to great effect in advertising and film where the agenda is the manipulation of human emotions. It is often the pleasure derived from listening (even as children) that motivates us to become actively involved in participation; we want to create and produce that which we derive psychological benefit from and in that respect it is a vocational activity.

The degree to which we are able to maintain intrinsic motivation can ultimately determine how long we are able to commit to improving our skills. This is because intrinsic motivation governs our attitude which determines the quality of engagement.

Our attitude includes our beliefs about music and about ourselves: self-perception + self-esteem = self-efficacy. Self-efficacy is what you *know* you can do, i.e. what you know you can achieve in any particular domain. One of our most valued psychological conditions is the idea that we have choice and can determine what we do and how and when we do it. When we are inspired we feel intrinsically motivated to act, to do something towards fulfilling ourselves in a chosen area. The inspiration (meaning one's spirit is infused) may have come from an extrinsic source, but it becomes internalised which results in vocational learning and behaviour. Given these circumstances, why are we ever reluctant to engage in the very activity we have not only chosen, but often worked hard and 'suffered' for in order to participate? What is the source of apathy? I suggest that it's connected to our habit of separating and compartmentalising things including ourselves, so that when we 'finally' enter a desired arena we can become anxious and doubtful; feelings of isolation and inadequacy begin to develop and, although their source lies in the uncontrolled imagination, their undoubted power gives rise to a variety of escape mechanisms.

Valued emotions and psychological benefits are our principal motivators and self-efficacy plays a crucial role in the degree to which we can realise our potential (or part of it). However, belief itself isn't enough if one is incompetent; it has to be based on reality (actual ability, which is the meaning of self-efficacy), otherwise we are simply delusional; happy perhaps, but delusional nonetheless. However, together with ability it leads to higher levels of achievement because one feels equipped to handle challenges on both the level of competence and confidence. Conversely, lack of self-efficacy, even with oceans of ability, is highly demotivating and ultimately damaging.

Intrinsic motivation also results in informal practice. This is practice often called by another name – jam sessions and so on – because the connotation of practice doesn't sound particularly appealing. Research shows that the highest achieving music students engage in more informal practice, i.e. they manage to maintain their intrinsic motivation. The *sense* of freedom and choice are conditions that help to enhance and maintain intrinsic motivation.

Extrinsic motivation refers to factors that are external and non-musical – money, reward, people, and fear. (Motivating people are peers, teachers, parents.) These can be short-lived and, if they are, result in perfunctory performance, complacency and cynicism.

Extrinsic motivation can be crucial in childhood but still has to be *in addition* to some desire on the child's part. Encouragement is a crucial external motivator. There is a motivation cycle of reward, approval and achievement. Important rewards are often musical, social and financial, and mostly include approval, which is one of the most powerful human needs. It is a highly valued psychological benefit, and psychological benefits are our ultimate goal. The need for supportive feedback never leaves us; even negative feedback is confirmation of our existence, impact and inclusion.

Approval from peers during adolescence can be bewilderingly influential. The navigation of a shifting and sometimes unstable sense of identity has always been a source of vulnerability and doubt, even without the insidious pressures from social media which can alienate as well as connect and intensify feelings of inadequacy. For musicians, the need to maintain social recognition and respect from their peer group frequently inspires and motivates practice and progress. Admiration from the admired is always sought after in any discipline. In 'conservatory culture' there exists an elitism that can have a negative and harmful effect on performing confidence and erode a formerly positive outlook and sense of self-worth.

This is also true of competition which can work for and against motivation and attitude. For some, competition is inextricably linked to a fear of failure and many won't even enter into the arena to be judged. For others, the desire to outdo competition, although potentially negative, can be highly motivating albeit it with an unhealthy attitude, i.e. lacking an artistic vocational and intrinsic source. It can result in achievement, but at a cost if the outcome becomes more important than developing skills and artistic integrity.

In his book *Performing Confidence*, musician and psychologist Andrew Evans identifies psychological mechanisms of escape as reactions to spurious self-confidence. For example, in order to maintain a possibly delusional belief in our ability, we avoid ever putting it to the test and find a catalogue of excuses for not 'entering the arena' – reasons such as illness, lateness, unavailability, instrument failure etc. Or, in the face of negative criticism or even simply poor feedback, we assume philistinism on the part of others who fail to appreciate our true artistry.

Maintaining a possible illusion about one's level of ability can be a result of childhood experience and a condition that Evans describes as 'Spells and Curses'. This is where we have been overpraised as children and develop a wholly unrealistic evaluation of our skills or, conversely, been poorly criticised with a prediction that any meaningful achievement is unlikely or impossible. Both types of comments (which can be made quite carelessly) are internalised by children and become 'true' for them because they enter their belief system – their subconscious minds. Even if a child experiences a curse- and spell-free childhood, he can suffer from excessive expectation in the evidence-based world of exams and results – from parents, teachers and peers – which can be highly de-motivating because the emphasis is on measurable achievement and competition rather than aesthetic appreciation and meaningful development. This in turn can grow into a need for perfectionism which is also delusional, sometimes to the point of deep neurosis. This is when, as Sloboda says, 'All music becomes a source of anxiety'.[1] Reaching the highest levels of performance, success requires a combination of many motivational factors, extrinsic sources of which become internalised and, therefore, *intrinsic* as

1 Exploring The Musical Mind

we develop. Musical activity can then become part of our true and stable identity.

Expectancy value theory was developed for general educational purposes and was more recently applied to music. It applies to both intrinsic and extrinsic motivation and measures the importance of personal values regarding any endeavour with expectations about what might be involved in carrying it out. As with all research of this type, it shows results from statistical studies that have been undertaken over measured time in order to identify behavioural and psychological traits that would appear common to most participants. These studies are valuable and can be helpful, especially in order to gain some degree of objectivity in what can feel to be, at times, a somewhat immersive subject. There is little point in reiterating the theory here, but together with Mastery and Helpless Orientation it is eruditely explained in *Psychology for Musicians* by Lehmann, Sloboda and Woody.

III. Emotion and Imagination

Desire springs from emotion and emotion is the conduit into the subconscious. It is the subconscious mind which can be likened to quantum mechanics in terms of personal and universal creation. It does what it is told, but it needs telling and reminding repeatedly. Each individual subconscious mind is part of what Jung described as the collective unconscious. It is a thinking substance that can be brought into physical existence deliberately. To achieve this one has to have a focused desire, which inevitably results in an emotional response which in turn causes feeling. This is the world of science, physics and measurable rationale. The substance measured is vibration of which all the physical world consists. We could equate it:

> Desire = emotion = feeling vibration = alignment = result (manifestation).

The difference between emotion and feeling is that emotion is mostly an involuntary reaction that is experienced at a physical level and usually in the lower body which may then travel elsewhere (crying, vomiting etc.,). Emotions cause biochemical reactions in the body and originally helped our species to survive by producing the necessary hormones. They are more primal than feelings in the way that they alter our physical state. Feeling is more subtle, meaningful and intense and results from the mind's interpretation of emotion. It is also the creative force because its fusion of thought and emotion – both powerful forces in their own right – produces the dynamic vibrational field that determines one's reality at any given time. Feeling is the secret.

> *It (mathematics) is both a mental construct and an integral part of the phenomenal universe because consciousness projects itself first into the mind, and then into the matter of the external world. The natural laws that determine how the phenomenal universe functions are an aspect of the universal consciousness that imposes order on the phenomenal universe so that life is possible.*
>
> — Michael Bradford – Consciousness: The New Paradigm

The subconscious mind is directed by the conscious mind, making the control of one's thoughts of paramount importance because thoughts create things. We imagine that our thoughts are private, but they are not. They can be felt; they transmit, connect and inform the thinking substance which realises them. This happens all of the time and is mostly unconscious and haphazard. By practising the control of our thoughts we can create the experiences we desire.

The universe can only expand and grow (thus far); it reproduces constantly and we can either co-create with it by engaging with the process of manifestation, or we can live in oblivion and experience the world of circumstance as and when it happens. The discipline of thought control is the biggest obstacle; or perhaps, the largest obstacle is believing that it is even possible. To accept that our mind is part of one far greater than itself and one which seeks to express itself in form is not easy, but it's no less true for that. We are here to develop the consciousness of the universe.

Everything depends on attitude towards self; it is the necessary condition by which our goals are achieved. The Law of Attraction is also known as the

Law of Assumption – they are the same. The Law of Assumption is entirely dependent on the imagination because imagination creates, manifests and brings thinking substance into physical being. To deliberately employ this law we must imagine and explore a new concept of ourselves, the person we aspire to be, what/whoever that is. The key is to assume, through imagination, that this concept alread exists.

Manifestation

We live in a vibrational universe. Nothing affects our vibrational levels more than our emotions. The way we feel is infinitely more powerful than the way we think and the truth of this is obvious with a moment of reflection; otherwise we would all be athletic teetotal vegan gods, studying literature, maths, art, and string theory.

Emotion is inextricably linked to intuition, which by its very nature functions on feeling. What is a 'hunch' but something one feels, yet is unable to explain rationally (with the conscious mind)? Intuition is teaching from within. If we learn to trust, tune in and be aware we can rely on and even live by it. In his book *Three Magic Words*, philosopher, mystic and author U.S. Anderson writes:

> 'We are using intuition to cover a good deal more than the occurrence of "hunches." Under intuition we are classifying all the mysterious and apparently unexplainable phenomena which pass largely unnoticed in our world: clairvoyance, thought transference, materializing and dematerializing objects,

> levitation, contact with the spirit world, in addition to an instinctive grasp of the laws of construction (such as in mathematics and music). Intuition describes our recognition and use of the great truth that mind is greater than matter and that the Universal Subconscious Mind contains the knowledge of all things and all times, is the substance from which everything is made, and is responsive to thought and desire.'

There is a level at which we *know.* Sometimes we know that we know, but mostly we don't. Again, repetition and practice are required, but are never more rewarding. Our emotions act like a barometer measuring our vibrational level. The better we feel, the higher (more rapid) the level and this is where the art/science of manifestation can be deliberately employed. The world that we experience exists as a result of our perception. Everything is a vibrational result or 'reality'. We only experience anything physical because our vibrational levels match. A chair is not a chair to another set of photons/electrons and only we, as humans, can exercise control over our vibrational level, because we are conscious and able to expand and raise our consciousness. In doing so, we are able to create and manifest anything that we desire and are prepared to focus our developing consciousness on.

Music is invisible as itself. The score is not the music, yet we readily accept its existence, its reality, and its language. Further, musicians surrender and engage the larger part of their lives, their energy, and their passion to it. By playing (with) music we bring it into the dimensional realm which we can readily experience. It can be heard and felt and, although feeling isn't generally classified as one of the five senses, it is the gateway to the sixth sense which is the transitional step towards the invisible world. In other words, emotion and subsequent feeling are, potentially, highly creative.

This brings us to the heart of the subject of manifestation and creating the experiences we wish to have. I'll start with a very simple example, followed by an explanation of its meaning with how and why it works.

> You would like more money. You think that if you had more, you would feel secure, free, intense relief and so on. If you really imagine

> this state so deeply that you can physically feel it, you can't fail to notice the alteration in your condition.
>
> The next thought is that *if* you had more money, *this* is how it would feel.
>
> The truth is that the money will manifest only if the feeling state exists already. You have to operate in the present tense.
>
> This is the practice; this is the repetition. This is how the world of vibration works. The difference in recent years is that quantum physics enables it to be measured and proven, and the rationalism of the western world loves measurement, evidence and dimensional 'reality'.

A strong influence during the past fifteen years has been an increased awareness in the Law of Attraction, especially since the publication of *The Secret* in 2002 by Rhonda Byrne. It's a book designed for mass appeal and, although she is the author, it's replete with 'pop-ups' quoting other people past and present. In terms of readability and sales it continues to be a huge success, but the degree of success experienced by its millions of readers is relatively limited. In it we are guided to 'ask, accept, receive'. This is extremely difficult for most people because the concept of acceptance conflicts with all that we think we know and, try as we might, it simply isn't strong enough; there's too much room for doubt which dilutes the necessary feeling. To create the required intensity we must *assume,* we must occupy the state of having already received or accomplished the desired condition and *stay there.* This is the way to use the imagination consciously and deliberately and the most efficient form of practising this is in meditation. The Law of Assumption is a more accurate title to describe how to engage in deliberate manifestation; the Law of Attraction operates by default constantly.

To give an example of how the power of assumption can be applied in our daily reality, the experience of teaching is among the clearest because we have all experienced it from both perspectives. We all teach by example and those actively involved in education ought to be engaged in empowering students by assisting them in the discovery of their own ability and potential by *removing any obstacles that might be blocking it.* When teachers *assume* the student's ability (while also catering for the input that they need) in the sense that they make their assumption apparent, the response is not only always positive, but often remarkable in terms of results. This partly arises from the desire to please and from the consequent approval, but the power of assumption from the teacher causes *an extraordinary and reflective power of assumption from the student – about themselves.* Confidence soars and with it their true capacity for achievement can be realised and expressed. This is an example of performance from both teacher and student. Teachers have to perform and, irrespective of the subject, are expecting their students to perform also. In the case of musicians this expectation might be intensified, but the approach and solution are essentially the same. Many lecturers and even one-to-one teachers suffer from anxiety at the prospect of having to step up to the mark and publicly convince others that they are experts in whatever field they might be holding forth on. And here the power of assumption operates again. Lecturers/teachers manifest ability just as students can, when they assume their own ability and expertise.

There is no such thing as empty space. 'Space' is full of intelligent matter, continually moving through form, into form, and out of form. That includes us. We are a vibrational field, as all things are. Our world operates on the same level as we do, which is why we can experience it. The things we want exist, but maybe at a different frequency which is why we don't experience them. Our emotional state creates a feeling state which in turn produces a vibrational one. It cannot not do this; it's doing it now. By taking control of this we can determine our three-dimensional reality which occurs through the alignment of vibrational fields. When they match, the fourth dimension materialises into the third, and we can see it, spend it, eat it, wear it. The strength of the emotional condition and the consequent feeling and vibrational field with which we want to match and manifest is dependent on and produced by the intensity of our desire, the capacity of our imagination and the strength of our feeling.

The artist is identified here as one whose attitude toward all things is creative rather than competitive. Competition is an ego-driven desire to conquer, to win, and to be better than others. Winning is more important than personal growth and real achievement; the temporary victory is fired by the need for superiority and approval. This need follows the same pattern as any physical body: birth, growth, decay, death.

The very nature of life itself is, essentially, expansion and creation. The universe cannot help but grow continually – weeds grow through asphalt. We either try to kill plants or cultivate them; the same can be said for people, ideas, art, and music. Whatever form creation takes, we, as humans, adopt an attitude to it; we want either more or less. We are all creators and being unconscious doesn't impede our default creative capacity. The world (we think) we know is our creation, most of which is conditioned and 'accidental'. Hence we feel victimised by circumstance, which renders us helpless, hopeless and reactionary.

We can choose to create with consciousness and deliberation, or without either. This decision can only be made with the awareness that there is even a choice.

Feelings differ from emotion in that they result from the fusion of the other two.

Thought = intellect

Emotion = body

Feeling = both

It is the feelings that vibrate in the quantum field that create our world. To control feelings, we must begin with thought. It is not the events and circumstances that occur in our lives that matter, but our reactions to them. Most of these reactions are automatic, habitual, and to some degree unconscious. To break the habit requires 1) changing our thinking so that 2) our emotional response shifts or ceases, and 3) the unwanted feelings don't appear.

All events are neutral. They are given meaning by the imposition of human values and consequent emotional responses. In other words, our experience is caused by our thoughts and imagination – not the other way round. We are the cause, and if we suffer from any effects it is because we have failed to realise this. Imagination is the key to liberation.

> *When you understand the redemptive power of imagination you hold in your hands the key to the solution of all your problems. Every phase of your life is made by the exercise of your imagination. Determined imagination alone is the means of your progress. It is the beginning and the end of all creating.*
>
> — Neville Goddard

To recognise the guidance that is available constantly is to gain insight into the meaning of co-creating. The subconscious mind is infinitely more powerful than the conscious mind. It is part of the quantum field of energy by which and through which all things are made. It is a law which can be harnessed or violated (ignored).

Consciousness is the only reality. In his book *Consciousness: The New Paradig'*, Michael Bradford explores and fuses science, spirituality and Indian philosophy, and explains quantum processes with great depth and clarity. (For that level of scientific detail, go to chapter 7 of his book.)

> *Quantum Theory has shown that consciousness, through the act of observation, forces sub-atomic particles to abandon their immaterial potential state and actually exist with a physical form at a particular location. How can consciousness be just a by-product of physical matter when it causes matter to actually exist with form and position? If consciousness is not a by-product of material processes then it must have an independent existence of its own. And since it can force matter to exist in actual physical*

state, it must be regarded as more 'real' than matter.

— Michael Bradford

Manifestation is unavoidable; we are surrounded by it and, in the case of excess conflict, worry, and so on, we are even suffocated by it, but mostly lack the ability to change it. The arrangement of particles in the quantum domain creates matter. If they are not arranged deliberately, they will be imperceptible – but that doesn't mean non-existent. The same is true for the arrangement of the mind which, to manifest what is desired, relies on the concept of oneself. This is what is meant by alignment; it's how magnetism works. Again, to manifest and receive anything desired, it is absolutely vital to maintain the feeling that it has already happened. This is what imagination is for; it creates and manifests. Some people call it God.

Because the attention of this book is focused primarily on musicians and musical performance, it might be useful to relate this information from that perspective.

Resonance is a natural occurrence that we all share. It is also a physics-based theory that explains the law and how to use it.

The word resonance means the reinforcement of sound by reflection, or the synchronous vibration of a neighbouring object. Musical instruments are set into vibration at their natural frequency when a person interferes with the object by direct contact which places energy into the instrument. This input of energy rearranges the particles and forces the object into vibrational motion at its natural frequency. The most interesting feature of resonance is that when one object is vibrating at the same frequency as another, the second object will begin vibrating seemingly spontaneously.

In physics, there is a popular experiment that demonstrates the exact way in which this works. A tuning fork is mounted on a sound box and placed on a table. A second tuning fork, which sounds at the same frequency, is placed on a table next to the first. Both tuning forks are stationary with no audible vibration.

The first tuning fork is struck with a rubber mallet and begins to vibrate at its natural frequency. These vibrations cause the sound box and the air inside to vibrate at the same frequency. Surrounding air particles are set into vibrational motion, also at the same vibrational frequency, and it becomes audible.

As the air particles around the first fork begin vibrating, the pressure waves that this creates begin to impact the second fork. Since those sound waves share the same natural frequency the second fork begins vibrating. This is an example of resonance: one object begins vibrating at the same natural frequency as a second object and forces that second object into vibrational motion that is in alignment. What does this have to do with manifestation? Everything.

You are just like the tuning fork. You carry a vibration that matches your thought and feeling states. The things that you want to experience in life are the same, and they carry their own distinct frequency. Because you don't have these things in your life, it can be concluded from the given experiment that you and those things are undetectable to one another. You aren't carrying the same vibrational frequency. In other words, what you want can't recognise or detect your vibration so that it can reach you. It is as if there is a dark tunnel between you and these things and, unless you light the path with your frequency, there is no way of one knowing the other is there.

Take a moment to imagine you are the first tuning fork in the experiment. Now imagine that you want to attract a large sum of money into your life. This large sum of money is the second tuning fork. You both exist in the same place, but you don't see or hear each other; you are literally unaware of each other's presence, although you could reach out and touch if you only knew the other was there. You can only become detectable if you strike your own abundance/ wealth tuning fork, which in turn causes the money tuning fork to make the same sound. When that happens, resonance has taken place and you are able to perceive the other's existence as physical reality. You are aware of the money that is a part of your reality, and it is aware of you, which completes the manifestation.

> *If you want to find the secrets of the universe, think in terms of energy, frequency and vibration.*
>
> — Nikola Tesla

Manifestation is recognising something through the senses that is perceived by the mind and noticed through awareness, i.e. making visible something that 'appears' to be invisible. Anything we don't notice, perceive or recognise, and is therefore not a part of our lives, we quickly and naively assume to not exist.

But imagine that everything you want is right in front of you; you simply don't see and hear it because your vibration is not a match. So, how can you consciously control the resonance that you project so you can perceive the reality of what you want?

Your vibrational frequency is your state of being. Your signature frequency is a combination of your thoughts, emotions and feelings. The waves created from these three things combine to form a standing wave that pulses and radiates your vibration and matches it with similar frequencies. This creates your perceived reality. Most importantly, all frequencies that can exist already do. All frequency combinations of all possible realities that can exist do co-exist simultaneously, right now in this moment. When you shift your thoughts, emotions, and feelings you alter your frequency or state of being. Once this happens you experience a different reality. The Law of Resonance is quite literally the law that determines how everything is in your physical reality.

Rollin McCraty is the director of the HeartMath Institute (www.heartmath.org) and has conducted research for well over twenty years into how thoughts and emotions are affecting ourselves and others. He and his team research the intelligence of the heart, its power over the brain and the effect that it has on our own experience and that of others.

> "It is important to consider what our emotions are contributing to our environment and to other people. Our research and its applications can help people create a positive emotion-based environment that has real effects on physiology."

McCraty said that the true nature of human emotion is one of care and love. He said HeartMath's and others' research shows that, by focusing on these core emotions, it can enhance one's connection with others, and that this connection extends far beyond the individual. Results from research at the HMI assert that the heart emits electromagnetic fields that alter according to your emotions and that the field can be measured feet away from the body. Negative emotion can produce chaos in the nervous system. The heart has a system of neurons with both short and long term memory, and their signals, when sent to the brain, impact emotional experience. The heart transmits more information to the brain than conversely, and creativity, problem solving and decision making are all enhanced by the heart's intelligence.

Morphic Resonance

In *Consciousness: The New Paradigm*, Michael Bradford devotes a section of chapter 7, 'Consciousness and Modern Science', to the subject of morphic resonance (a scientifically broader perspective to the resonance discussed in the previous section). He does so largely by quoting from a book by Rupert Sheldrake published in 1981, *A New Science of Life: The Hypothesis of Morphic Resonance.*

Bradford draws parallels between Sheldrake's hypothesis and more current thinking regarding human consciousness. He identifies the links but, more interestingly, the differences.

Sheldrake writes:

> "The morphic fields of mental activity are not confined to the inside of our heads. They extend far beyond our brain through intention and attention. We are already familiar with the idea of fields extending beyond the material objects in which they are rooted: for example, magnetic fields extend beyond the surfaces of magnets; the earth's gravitational field extends

> far beyond the surface of the earth, keeping the moon in its orbit; and the fields of a cellphone stretch out far beyond the cell itself. Likewise the field of our minds extend far beyond our brains."

Bradford explains how Sheldrake applied the theory of how information, communication, habit and, specifically, memory operate in a variety of living organisms – plants, rats, pond life, trees etc., and, inevitably, humans. The suggestion is that memory and therefore habit can be and probably are stored and shared from outside the brain, and that a pre-existing set of patterns can impose processes. This 'resonance' goes some way to explaining dream content and psychic phenomena, including telepathy. It could also be linked to DMT activity in the brain.

Bradford explains the critical difference between Sheldrake's theory of morphic resonance and his own perception of it. It is that Sheldrake avoids mentioning the concept of an overriding intelligence, a cosmic force, that is responsible for the ultimate creation. Something has to assemble the components into structural matter. A field, or fields, of memories and habits cannot do that. Sheldrake avoided the word consciousness. (It was the early '80s and science was still governed by a wholly materialistic paradigm of reality. Although this is changing, it's still proving slow in some quarters, given the evidence now available.)

> *The chilly reception that his theories have received is a clear indication of how far the orthodox scientific community still have to change before a concept such as prana shakti will be seriously considered.*
>
> – Michael Bradford

Visualisation

The human brain likes to look at pictures. Given a tome to read, even on a subject of interest, the tendency is to detect the inclusion of visual aids. We don't have to be art lovers to be visually stimulated – a fact that the world of advertising demonstrably exploits. How often have we noticed an advertisement and not understood the content? The subconscious mind knows instantly and looks for the match without any help from the conscious mind which is still unable to identify the message.

Mind-mapping is the art of absorbing information quickly and efficiently through visualisation. Instead of taking linear notes one does what the brain defaults to when relaxed in a confined environment – doodles, scribbles freely without constraint. It has been proven that this technique of, say, taking lecture notes is 100% more productive in long-term memory gain than any form of linear note-taking (including recording which requires no conscious manual effort and no mental effort at all in most cases).[1] Through the deliberate application of the brain's instinct for pictures conveying information, one can not only increase absorption and understanding, but drastically reduce the time spent revising in the attempt to commit data to memory. Here is Tony Buzan's definition of the mind map:

The Mind Map is an expression of Radiant Thinking and is therefore a natural function of the human mind. It is a powerful graphic technique which provides a universal key to unlocking the potential of the brain. The Mind Map can be applied to every aspect of life where improved learning and clearer thinking will enhance human performance. The Mind Map has four essential characteristics:

---

1 Tony Buzan – The Mind Map Book 1993

a) The subject of attention is crystallised in a single image.

b) The main themes of the subject *radiate* from the central image as branches.

c) Branches comprise a key image or key word printed on an associated line. Topics of lesser importance are also represented as branches attached to higher level branches.

d) The branches form a connected nodal structure.

In chapter 24 of the same book he lists the optimum times for revision in order to commit information to long term memory:

For a one hour period of study:

*After 10 minutes – take a 10 minute review

*After 24 hours – take a 2 – 4 minute review

*After a week – take a 2 minute review

*After a month – take a 2 minute review

*After 6 months – take a 2 minute review

*After a year – take a 2 minute review

He suggests mind-mapping what you can remember before consulting your original for best results. 20 – 22 minutes looking at pictures over a year is efficient. It also relates directly to chapter 1 of this book.

The other form of visualisation doesn't involve any manual dexterity – just the imagination. It is often referred to as creative visualisation and, in her book of that title, Shakti Gwain writes:

> "Creative visualisation is the technique of using your imagination to create what you want in your life... there is nothing new, strange or unusual about it; you are already using it every day, every minute in fact. It is your natural power of imagination, the basic, creative energy of the universe which you use constantly, whether or not you are aware of it."

This was written in 1978 when this area of thought was considered 'new-age' and alternative as opposed to an area of scientific excitement as it is seen today.

The techniques for visualisation are the same as for manifestation – how to make the invisible visible – and is another term for aligning vibrational states in order to realise them. Some people find the creation of clearly defined images difficult to achieve, but that need not arrest the process entirely. Visualisation works because of its capacity to create an emotional response followed by the electromagnetic *feeling* which, with repetition, can be sustained, thereby radiating the necessary vibration seeking matching particle waves. The difference between visualisation and manifestation is really one of degree. Visualisation is a tool, an aid to intensify the process of creation, but if it's a struggle which causes resistance it will be counterproductive. Manifestation is the ability to occupy the state of the fulfilled wish and to fully assume its reality. It is more powerful than visualisation alone because of the strength of its presence and the absence of any wish for a future condition. The most important point is that it is the subconscious mind that is being re-programmed which is why it is necessary to be as relaxed as possible, to enjoy the experience, to play with it, and to practice repeatedly.

IV. Anxiety and Mind

Cause and Effect

The feeling of protection is the answer to fear. Regardless of age, circumstance, situation or agenda, this is always true. We tend to seek protection from without – to be rescued, gathered up and soothed with unconditional approval. Academically and commercially successful and respected adults can swiftly feel the desire for the 'ground to open up and swallow them' when their credibility and authority feel threatened. The need to disappear is followed by the need for reassurance and restoration. It is our base instincts that can cause the most distress, but they are controllable with the practice and repetition of instant remedies that can be applied in stressful situations.

In his lecture 'Hacking Your Consciousness Indian Style,'[1] (14th February 2016 at the IIC New Delhi), the mystic visionary, Kundalini authority and guru

Raja Choudhury (FN) demonstrates an immediately effective breathing technique that will alleviate anxiety in any situation. This is because it arrests the message from the lower (emotional) regions of the body to the reactive reptilian brain. These messages transmit fear, threat, flight and attack, most of which are superfluous and inappropriate responses. Before the flood of adrenalin disables us, he describes an instant breathing technique to stem the flow by controlling the heart rate which blocks the message. (This is how beta-blockers work.) We need these tools and practices in our daily lives to address any (potentially) stressful situation (Appendix 2).

Anxiety *can* spring from selfishness and vanity. This may be hard to believe, but understanding and accepting it is the path to the cure.

Thus far in this book I have been repeatedly referring to consciousness, imagination and the one mind that we all share – 'there is only one of us here'. The exploration and understanding of human consciousness is widely considered to be the principle scientific preoccupation of the twenty-first century. As early as 1922 Alice Bailey, in a series of lectures that she wrote and delivered in New York, suggests that man's self-consciousness limits rather than expands by causing a vanity and self-obsession that results in a sense of isolation, insecurity, and anxiety because we are unable to grasp our connection to everybody else and to the greater whole.

> "Self-centeredness, that cycle in which man is principally concerned with his own affairs, with that which primarily interests him, and lives his own intense, internal, vibratory life [makes us] only mentally interested in the things that are going on in the world. We remain wholly concerned with our own individual lives, primarily intent on comfort, pleasure, diversion and acquisition. Then we might progress to education, research, discovery and creation, but still principally for ourselves rather than through an awareness of the humanity of which we are a part."

She goes on to say,

> "Having learned to be intelligent units by means of [our] five senses and having expanded our consciousness, we reach a certain crisis. That of intelligent discrimination ... the discrimination

> which the self-conscious unit demonstrates – the conscious choice which we will be forced to utilise as the power of evolution drives us on to the point where we will learn to distinguish between the self and the not-self, between the real and the unreal, between the life within the form and the form which it uses, between the knower and that which is known. Here we have the whole object of evolution, the attainment of the consciousness of the real self through the medium of the not-self."

Selfishness and vanity are highly unattractive qualities, which therefore need defining for clarity. Anxiety always concerns oneself, even if you are anxious about another's behaviour; it is your response to it that is the cause. If your concern is about your own behaviour it is other people's responses to it – imagined or otherwise – that causes your anxiety.

Many people are anxious about being anxious – frightened of fear – and this holds more truth than is immediately apparent; it is the root of fear. If you are scared of tigers or snakes, it is not of these creatures themselves, but of how they might make you feel according to the risk involved. In other circumstances you might well rescue them. It is the potential effect on your emotional state that is fearful. I have said that emotions are far more powerful than thoughts and reason. Fear is not rational and so needs to undergo some scrutiny in order to reduce its impact.

The fear of fear is partly physical. Our bodies undergo fourteen physiological changes when we have a sudden shock, because the intelligence of the organism rapidly prepares for immediate danger by flooding itself with the necessary hormones to enable you to perform extraordinary physical feats beyond normal capability. Unless you have to flee from a wild tiger or lift a car to release your child, this huge surge of physical strength is so surplus to requirements that it can be debilitating, and the physical responses become a secondary reason for fear; you can feel your body losing control in a variety of areas – pulse, bladder, bowels, sweat glands, breath control, throat stricture etc. If you have a shock while driving, you barely need do more than make a slight movement of the wrist to restore you to safety, yet this adrenalin flood has to go somewhere.

If you are a performing musician, this is a potential 'disaster'. Your body deserts you just when you most need it to be poised, controlled and at your command. We will consider the musician, because the driver may well have narrowly escaped a life-threatening moment but the musician is engaged in a vocational activity which he has spent years developing and this is the moment he has been working towards. Assuming the performer has good self-efficacy and is well prepared, what happens in his thoughts, emotions and feelings?

The situation regarding lecturers and students (discussed in the previous chapter) can be likened to a musical performance and the audience. All artistic performers (actors, musicians, live artists) express reactions and opinions about 'the audience' and refer to it as a single entity irrespective of numbers. It's as if the audience has its own identity and collective reaction – and for the performer(s) it does. There is, inevitably, a significant difference between the solo artist and a group, but the fascinating fact is that in a collaborative performance the artists feel the same reaction to the audience *collectively.* Solo performers experience audience contribution and participation according to their own capacity to interact with it and for this they need empathy – possibly the first psychological construct to vanish when they feel anxious. Without it the audience inevitably becomes a projection of the performer's mental/emotional state and embodies the judgement and criticism that, in the case of a highly anxious artist, contribute to the cause of the anxiety from within. Performance anxiety stems from confronting one's own psychological state and realising how negative it is, except that it's an emotional realisation which is paralysing when facing an auditorium full of expectant people who are all reflections of oneself.

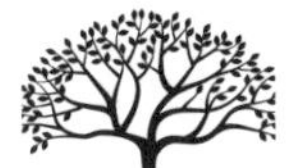

Thoughts attempt to identify causes such as fear of criticism, rejection, memory loss and general failure. Often, the final desperate consolation is that, however disastrous something is, it won't kill us. Absurd though it seems, this is the key to insight – the ultimate fear is death. If, as a performer suffering from anxiety, the impending occasion is only consoled by the extreme example of annihilation, about which we know very little, the two experiences must have something in common, however imaginary.

One of the principal causes of fearing death is the unknown. But a stronger cause is the fear of complete isolation. Now, you wouldn't know you were in complete isolation unless you were conscious of being so, and many people believe that consciousness ends with the physical body. For those people, fear of death is nonsensical, yet they still have it. Furthermore, what is so dreadful about being alone?

I suggest that the fear of isolation and all the associated 'causes' (rejection, judgement, criticism, failure) stem from lack of consciousness – deliberate, self-aware, internal consciousness. The experience of suddenly being *you,* all on your own with the expectation of accomplished artistic endeavour, can be overwhelming *if you don't know who you are.*

What does this mean? It means that you haven't spent time in your own mind with no distraction in order to explore and gradually discover what is in there, in the 'silence'.

The mind is too vast to easily contemplate, but there is only one and we all share it; except that, if you suffer from anxiety and fear it is because you haven't been sharing it. You have been selfish and vain, believing that you have a mind separate from everyone else's – of course it's terrifying! You against a hostile world that expects you to prove your tiny insignificant self in an entertaining and convincing manner.

There is a related condition in all strata of the corporate world (and artistic and every other) known as fraud syndrome. It occurs at every level, irrespective of rank and seniority, and is where employees (and bosses, most of whom are also employees) are permanently anxious that their incompetence will be discovered and ridiculed. Everyone believes that everyone else is confident and secure, yet it is quite possible that none of them are. There are even courses providing therapy to address what has, indeed, become a widespread syndrome.

Inadequacy lies at the root of all these expressions of self-doubt and unworthiness. We know that self-efficacy is when you have a clear and realistic knowledge of what you are capable of, and, while this is useful, it won't conquer anxiety of and by itself. Conversely, vanity is an acute sense of separateness; excessive pride in one's ability and power. It causes us to see the world as potentially hostile and threatening, creating obstacles to limit and frustrate us. And the world turns out to be exactly what we conceive it to be – as it always must.

The more opposition and competition we imagine, the more frantic and threatened we become, from which an absurd sense of responsibility and pathological feelings of isolation ensue. Truly exceptional artists know that they are co-creating with the universal mind of which we are all a part. The artist is identified here as one whose attitude toward all things is creative rather than competitive. Competition is an ego-driven desire to conquer, to win and to be better than others. Winning is more important than personal growth and real achievement; the temporary victory is fired by the need for superiority and approval. This need follows the same pattern as any physical body: birth, growth, decay, death.

The awareness and experience of co-creation fills one with an overwhelming sense of gratitude and awe from which a huge quantum field radiates, and with it an experience of deep humility. To cultivate an abiding sense of appreciation and gratitude is among the most rapid of mind changers. Even on a bad day (especially on a bad day), to make the effort to pause from all that's not going well and to notice what *is* creates a powerful shift in awareness and mood. For example (and if these suggestions are true), you can see; you can walk; you are dry/warm/ hydrated; you have an address; you're not in pain; food is available; choice exists.

> *It is through gratitude for the present moment that the spiritual dimension of life opens up.*
>
> — Eckhart Tolle

During the last few months of his life, the award-winning neurologist and author Oliver Sacks (1933 – 2015) wrote four essays on the subject of gratitude. He knew he was terminally ill with very little time left and spent his final months dwelling on the gift of life:

> "My predominant feeling is one of gratitude... I have been a sentient being, a thinking animal, on this beautiful planet, and that in itself has been an enormous privilege and adventure."

Oliver Sacks spent his life studying, treating and connecting with other people. He was also a musician and in his extraordinary book *Musicophilia* (Picador 2008) he describes repeatedly the capacity of music to heal, to relieve isolation and to create an awareness and feeling of oneness, empathy and sharing. All of the people, the people he discusses in this book, were suffering – they were his patients, but through him managed to traverse thresholds of musical experience that many of us still struggle with. It is, above all, the realisation of human and spiritual connection and unity that has to be the focus of our time at all levels of human activity.

These are the psychic conditions that result in an authentic and integral performance of any kind. It can only happen when the focus of attention is shifted and broadened, so that not everything is about 'you'. The audience are a part of you; they don't inflict suffering and torment onto any artist – quite the reverse. It is the ego, the small surface self, that has to be dealt with and removed. It is the root cause of all fear because it is completely delusional, proud and stubborn.

In Part II we will examine the means for transformation. To close this chapter we will consider meditation, which is the most effective and long-lasting practice to effectively reduce and dispel anxiety. As the opening of this book states, if we want to change our experience we must begin with our thoughts because thoughts create things. Meditation is the most efficient method for achieving this because we go to the 'world within' and stay there. We gradually discover what is really happening in there and, eventually, who we really are. Once you know who you are, you cannot be threatened, because nothing that is real can be threatened.

Therein lies your peace.

— A Course in Miracles.

Meditation

Meditation is a practice and a discipline that will gradually disperse the egotistical sources of social and performance anxiety. Identifying sources of anxiety and low confidence is the first of several steps, but isn't the cure which is what we are all looking for; we want to know *how* to alleviate and dispel the debilitating experience of anxiety, and that defines the purpose of this book: to assist in identifying the cause and then to navigate the myriad of possible cures which can feel so overwhelmingly diverse that they generate further anxiety in case the wrong path is chosen and/or we can't manage it or afford it. The truth is that anyone can both manage and afford it (it's free) and throughout these chapters we are recognising the similarities, the links and the truth that binds it all together so as to simplify the approach to inner liberation. The only 'wrong path' is to ignore it. The purpose of choosing alchemy as the core practice is because of its clarity in demonstrating correspondences between all levels of existence – the seen and the unseen – and also because of its ancient wisdom in knowing that the consciousness of the practitioner (artist) impacts the substance (art) as does the recipient (audience). When these three elements dynamically interact they create a unified performance. This is true sharing, the absence of which is the root cause of anxiety, and it is evident globally, politically and personally. In Sam Harris's latest book, *Waking Up*, he writes,

> "It is true that meditation requires total acceptance of what is given in the present moment. If you are anxious before a speech, become willing to feel the anxiety fully, so that it becomes a meaningless pattern of energy in your mind and body. Embracing the contents of consciousness in any moment is a very powerful way of training yourself to respond differently to adversity ... truly accepting them as transitory appearances in consciousness. Only [this] gesture opens the door to wisdom and lasting change."

Paradoxically, the subject of meditation can itself be the source of some level of anxiety. There appear to be so many techniques and practices all purporting to be 'the way' to enlightenment. The fact is that most of us aren't seeking enlightenment; we just want to stop worrying to the extent that we're unable to demonstrate our abilities and *share* them with others.

Meditation is not mysterious, difficult or esoteric. It can be done anywhere, anytime, for a couple of minutes or as long as twenty (or as long as you like). It need cost nothing and it's not possible to fail at it. There is a rapid experience of relief and calm and a plethora of guidance available. (See Appendix 2 for suggested techniques.)

There is a 'fear exercise' I introduce at some stage of a meditation course, which is designed to demonstrate fear's illusory nature. After an introductory relaxation period, I suggest that the students summon either a memory or an imaginary forthcoming event/ performance which feels highly stressful. Then, when they've had time and encouragement to make this as real as possible by means of feeling, instead of working on controlling and reducing the fear, they are asked to strengthen it, to increase the feeling of fear and trepidation as much as possible even though it is extremely unpleasant. There is palpable tension, but without fail they are unable to sustain it – not because it's so dreadful, but because it evaporates. They actually go through the fear of fear to discover that it is not real. In meditation we explore the world within and eventually discover that our idea of ourselves is not real either. The small, over-reacting, dramatic, fearful egoic self is unable to withstand close scrutiny, quietness, stillness, and lack of distraction because it thrives on their absence. Eckhart Tolle (*The Power of Now*) calls this the 'pain body' and it is indeed the world of pain and suffering. It is this surface self that is fearful, threatened, lacking confidence and self-esteem, *fraudulent* and extremely anxious. It fears being discovered and ultimately discarded. In meditation we learn to discard it. The root cause of 'fraud syndrome' is itself fraudulent, making the entire condition an illusion. The practice of meditation confronts and removes these obstacles and helps to create a world that 'your mind wants live in.'

The psychological experiences described above are most commonly assigned to adolescence, which is notoriously a period of transition, identity exploration and rejection of established values and expectations. The brain continues to grow until the age of twenty-five, so that the adolescent brain undergoes many years of potential 'identity shifts' with feelings of transience and instability. The gradual realisation that our beliefs and reactions are not actually our own, but planted onto us by parents, teachers, and other significant adults, leads us to react, sometimes aggressively, in an attempt to discover what it is that we consider to matter and to be true. Inevitably, this leads to the idea of free will, because the adolescent brain insists on it, i.e. it insists on *feeling* as if it is making its own choices and life decisions.

In many respects adolescence is comparable to early childhood in that it is a period of exploration and often quite radical change. The huge difference is the levels of awareness and of the inhibition discussed in chapter I. Both of these impact the capacity to take responsibility and to embrace independence and there is, inevitably, a conflict between the desire to break free and the often equally powerful one to remain protected; it is quite possible to experience both within the hour. The deciding factor will usually be a sense of reward – teenagers love rewards and pay-offs. These frequently manifest in the form of peer approval and, in second place, adult approval. This is because of a fluctuating sense of identity which requires acknowledgement from Without.

Free will is a notion; it seduces us into a belief that more choice and greater freedom will result in fulfilment. The fact is that we don't like too much 'free will', or freedom of any kind, and we dislike too much choice although we are continually led to believe otherwise.

The illusion of free will (which, according to Sam Harris, is itself illusory) causes consideration of issues such as responsibility and morality. But where do they come from? Do they truly belong to us or did we simply adopt them without challenge? Initially, yes, of course we did, but at the point of challenge, when we go shopping around for alternative viewpoints, doctrines and practices, very often it is little more than swapping one for another, rather like returning an item to a store in exchange for another one – try it and see. All of this is inevitable in teenage years, but should develop into a more profound perspective, into what is meant by identity and the freedom to choose it. Rather than pursue a fixed 'self' which is recognisable and with which we are stuck forever, self-perception can *always* be a work in progress – fluid, malleable, and capable of change.

This is not confined to adolescence; shaping and channelling the true self is an activity for life which relates to the subject of play (see chapter I). Total freedom is paralysing and free will doesn't really exist; we haven't got it and don't want it. We want, need and fantasise about inspiring parameters which we excitedly, artistically and passionately respond to with our creative and liberated minds. The freedom that we do have is the choice concerning our state of mind, our personal evolution, and how we wish to experience the world; and we are able to gain most insight and control of these in meditation and in art. The artist is always working within constraints, and their freedom lies in the fact that these constraints are personally chosen and self-imposed; they emerge from within, are not exerted from without. This is precisely what makes it a creative and contextually appreciated act; artists cannot create from *nothing,* nor can meditators operate without a mind. Both disciplines result in freedom having arisen from the freedom to choose to engage. Insight into how things work mechanically, scientifically and spiritually enables us to make choices and to see that we can be the authors of our experience and that the free will that we do have is to make this choice. To have recognised this and ignored it is the only cause for blame and retribution.

The promotion of meditation is happening the world over and most notably in the west simply because in the east they've known and practised it for thousands of years so have no need for to promote it; it's a way of life. What makes it especially notable in Europe and America is the people who are doing the promoting being predominantly physicists, cosmologists and neuroscientists – the world of academic identity, mostly male, and certainly from a highly rationalist scientific background. In chapter VII we will meet John Hagelin who, in any hour long lecture on some aspect of quantum superstring theory, unashamedly explains that he plans to get through the physics section as fast as possible in order to dwell on the more exciting subject of transcendental meditation. It's a joy to witness.

There is well documented evidence on the science of meditation which is the measurable benefit enjoyed by regular practitioners. Exhaustive research into brain activity using all available scanning technology (see Shamatha Project, chapter VIII) reveals that in practising meditators there is increased activity in regions directly correlated with decreased anxiety and depression together with increased pain tolerance. There is also improvement in memory, planning, and *empathy.* Actual brain size is affected in terms of more grey matter which impacts learning capacity and emotional control. It improves blood pressure, heart rate and immune function as well as alleviating conditions such as psoriasis and IBS. This research is best known for being conducted at Stanford and

Harvard universities, but it is an ongoing project all over the world. Meditation practices have now been adopted by such diverse institutions as the Marines, corporate businesses, primary schools (very few) and financial marketers. Far from any longer being an esoteric Eastern phenomenon, Western rationalists have witnessed these results and want them as soon as possible!

Meditation is not so much something we *do* as something we allow to occur and make a frequent habit of. It is the art of observation, of watching ourselves think. Gradually we become more identified with the watcher than the thinker and curious about who that is. Imagine sitting in a valley by a stream and noticing all the detail around you – water, rocks, fish, other people, your own feet – with your thoughts and opinions scattered here and there. Then, climbing up the hill behind and from the top gazing out around the panorama and not only seeing vastly more than before but also grasping the context and perspective of where you were. The practice is to occupy that position, to be high up on the hill as the observer of our own reality. Eventually, it becomes a part of life, a state that need never desert us but which varies in degrees of awareness and intensity.

It's all too easy to be dismissive of current thinking (lack of), concentration spans, attention deficit, and lowering of standards, but we need to navigate the world that we actually live in. Weighty discourse on the Upanishads, the Sutras, and the Emerald Tablet are not helpful to most of us. In the past, alchemists knew about the *essence* of conscious creation, but they couldn't measure and prove it at quantum level as they can now. The scientific truth may have been felt intuitively and intensely in ancient Eastern wisdom, but not understood intellectually in terms of particle physics. Our brains have to withstand a daily deluge of information that can be a struggle to avoid let alone focus on and it is evitable that attention and concentration suffer as a result. We need *distilled* guidance that is intelligible, useable, reliable, and efficient. If any suggested practice seems too demanding to incorporate into daily life with relative ease, ultimately it will be unsustainable, of no benefit at all, and possibly adding to a sense of inadequacy (Appendix 4 – The Wisdom of Brevity).

The neuroplasticity of the brain enables it to create new synaptic pathways throughout life and into old age. Certain disciplines such as music, art and sport, all of which are harmoniously repetitive, result in new brain pathways that can be deliberately manipulated in order to replace former emotional responses and beliefs. Musicians and artists are highly predisposed to the experience of meditation. They know the feeling of being 'in the zone', of being wholly present in the creation of sound and structure, with little if any intrusion from the outside world. Theirs *is the real world* – connecting and communicating through its creative expression. The experience is sensational and spiritual all at once and, inevitably, we want to go back there to repeat it and to *share it.* This experience so often occurs away from public performance of any sort, i.e. even an individual lesson. All instrumental tutors have been told how much better it was previously and I daresay they've all also said it themselves. The frustration creates tension and it can be downhill from there. This is really the crux of the matter. How do we reliably reproduce, in any sort of public, our capacity to transcend the psychological and emotional constraints *that we feel to be imposed from the outside*? The hardest step is the first one which, is to accept that the imposition cannot be from the outside and that all causes are internal. Hard it may be, but intuitively we know it. The next step is to understand that addressing the issue has to be done daily and in non-musical situations; nothing will ever change otherwise. The control that we aspire to in public must be exercised in private! This is a crucial point. Our solitary brilliance, *'zone'* and *'flow'* experiences are usually surprising and spontaneous occasions and as such are highly valuable and precious. But we need to learn how to create that state *at will* when we are alone, because if we can't do it then it won't happen elsewhere.

What, then, is that state? We can describe it as liberation, transcendence, pure connection, and more. Meditation enables us to practise occupying that state at will, without musical instruments or scores. The benefit is gradually felt in daily life through our changing reactions, increased tolerance and ability to deal with situations calmly. We must be clear about what it is that we are aspiring to in performance. It is not marvellous technique: technique doesn't communicate and cannot be addressed in performance; all of that work is done. Rather, it is all of the above – pure connection, freedom of expression, and the transcendence of technique. In performance we are, essentially, meditating – highly alert and feeling part of the greater whole. We aspire to perform from the top of the hill.

IV. Anxiety and Mind

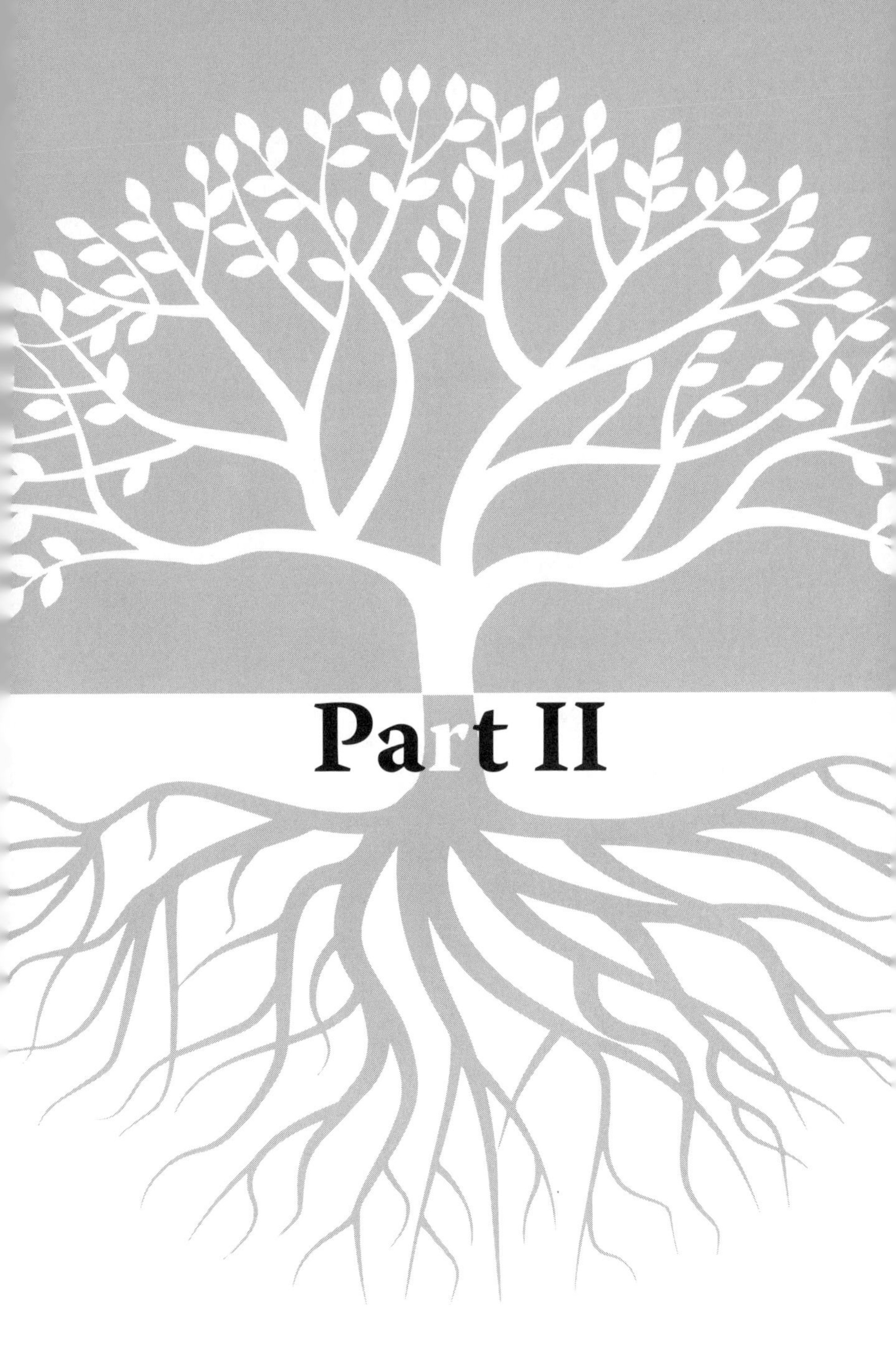

Part II

V. Background and Introduction to Alchemy

We live in an age of anxiety, insecurity and confusion. We also live in an age of transformation and change – globally, universally, and personally. Never has insight and understanding been more necessary to cultivate the inner changes that will enable us to navigate the dimensional movement that is affecting every aspect of our daily experience. It is little wonder that our symptoms are intensifying when the political (and therefore social) climate feels to be spiralling beyond comprehension. But all that is happening in the world is in response to that which is happening beyond the world: planetary cycles, dimensional shifts and electromagnetic forces that are mostly beyond our comprehension and control. These changes occur with or without human awareness. Increasing numbers of scientists, physicists, artists and spiritualists are talking and writing about various aspects of what is taking place in evolutionary terms and the definition 'spiritual science' is becoming widely used and accepted. In his most recent book *Waking Up*, Sam Harris doesn't discuss alchemy overtly, but his message refers to it obliquely. *Waking Up* is the perfect title to describe becoming conscious of what has always existed. Science and spirituality are no longer perceived as a duality and spirituality does not imply religion. Alchemy is the very epitome of spiritual science and existed long before the 300+ years of rationalist lateral progress intent on measuring and proving the nature of the physical world. It is the relationship between consciousness and matter and contains all of the guidance, answers and deliverance that we might ask for. The French alchemist, Jean Dubuis, wrote:

> 'Alchemy is the art of manipulating life and consciousness in matter, to help it evolve, or to solve problems of inner disharmonies.'
>
> — Hauck – *The Sorcerer's Stone.*

History and Principles

The Greeks and Egyptians travelled, mixed between and among cultures, and developed the art of alchemy. The Greek God of alchemy was Hermes – a name so influential that it is part of our language even now: hermetically sealed (a direct alchemical reference); hermetic truth, also alluding to sealing and being impenetrable; even a courier company has adopted it as a message that your stuff is safe, it's sealed, contained, protected and cannot be contaminated.

Hermes is said to have written the core text for the understanding of alchemical philosophy. It is called *The Emerald Tablet* and is short but nonetheless profound. The first paragraph is the key. It reads:

> 'That which is Below corresponds to that which is Above, and that which is Above corresponds to that which is Below, to accomplish the miracle of the One Thing. And just as all things come from this One Thing through the meditation of One Mind, so do all created things originate from this One Thing through transformation.'

The Above is the heavens, sky, cosmos, universe, eternal landscape of the soul. The Below is earth, matter, bodies, the land of mortals, and physical form. These two correspond and combine to become *The One Thing*. Alchemists knew that all things are created by and from this One Thing, and this was known as The First Matter or Prima Materia. This First Matter expressed itself as a trinity, the concept of which is evident in many religions and spiritual practices. The ancient Sumerians believed in a triad of gods and divided the then known universe into three, which was overseen by Anu, Enlil and Enki. Later, the Babylonians adopted the Sumerian trinity although they conceived the three-in-one idea rather than distinct and separate deities: Nimrod, Semiramis and Tammuz – father/sun, mother/moon and son/earth – with the belief that Nimrod married his mother in order to acquire the all-seeing third eye through the son who united them into one god. They also adopted the hexagon as a symbol: one which continues to be a source of controversy and debate. Ancient Egyptians worshipped their divine trinity of Anun, Ra and Ptah – wind, sun and creation respectively. Later the Egyptians also revered the trinity of Osiris/father, Isis/mother and Horus/son. Hinduism is probably the oldest religion and had the triune doctrine long before Christianity was even founded. In the *Puranas* it is written that there is no real distinction between them although their three identities are Brahma, Vishnu and Shiva. In Ayurvedic medicine there are the three *Doshas* which identify body types reflecting the personality, thus enabling precise and holistic treatment. They are *vata, pitta* and *kapha* and determine diet, healing and behaviour. Then, of course, we have Christianity with the Holy Trinity of the Father, Son and Holy Spirit which unite to be the one God – the *One Thing.*

Alchemy has its three principles also. A principle is a fundamental truth or proposition that serves as the foundation for a system of belief, behaviour, or a line of reasoning. When the end of reasoning power is reached the foundation principle or truth is arrived at. There are three principles in alchemy that exist within everything – plants, rocks, animals, people – *everything* in creation. *Hermes Trismegistus* means 'the thrice great Hermes', which translates as Hermes in Greek, Mercury in Roman, and Thoth as the Egyptian counterpart – 'all the same guy', as Avery Hopkins explains in his lecture on operative alchemy. In *The Emerald Tablet* Hermes identifies the wisdom of the universe as comprising three parts: alchemy,

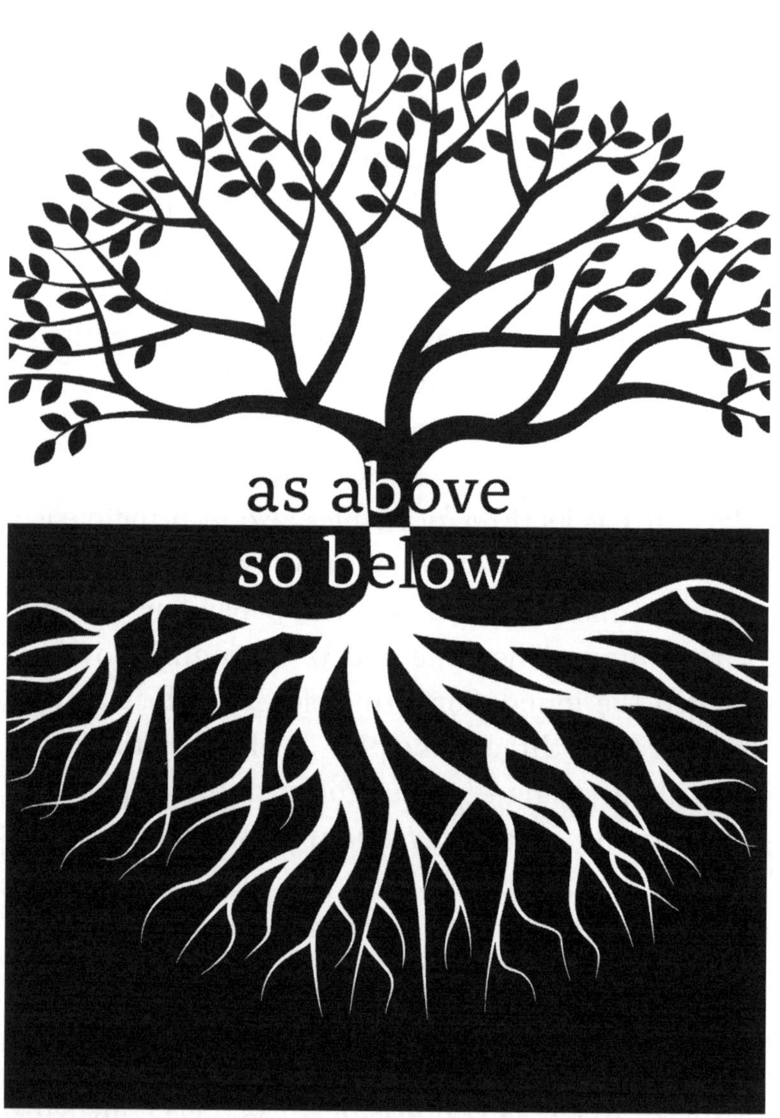

Figure 1

astrology and theurgy (divine magic) which refers to divine *work* – The Great Work – the only work and all that work should be (refer to chapter 1).

Alchemists used codes and ciphers to disguise this information partly because, centuries ago, particularly during the medieval and renaissance periods, it was a closely guarded secret for a variety of reasons, both personal and political.

The first of the three principles was labelled Sulphur, which was the code word for the soul. The second principle was known as Mercury, which was the code word for the spirit. The third was Salt, which was the code word for the body. The definition of a body is 'a material structure that gives concrete reality to something abstract' (Avery Hopkins, Philosopher and Practising Alchemist). Something abstract has to be an idea. Where do ideas originate? In the mind, which is the next principle. This is the spirit Mercury. The mind generates mental activity, and thoughts and ideas come from the mind. Therefore the body is simply structured thought patterns. The mind is defined as an inherent faculty of consciousness, which means consciousness inherently has the power to think. Thinking can be structured and those thoughts can be embodied to give concrete reality or appearance to an idea.

Soul	Sulphur	Consciousness
Spirit	Mercury	Mind
Body	Salt	Structured thought

Soul is the *actuating cause* of everything.

Above – Soul – Consciousness

Hermes/Mercury/Mind/Thought

Below – Body – Manifestation

Alchemy is the understanding of the relationship between consciousness and matter which are connected via the mind. It is the science of mind. Paracelsus, the most influential alchemist of the renaissance (1498 – 1541), was responsible for identifying the trinity of sulphur, mercury and salt; he added salt to represent the body (matter):

> 'Know then that all seven metals are born from a three-fold matter, namely, Sulphur, Mercury and Salt.....The soul, which indeed is Sulphur,

> unites these two contraries, the body and the spirit, and changes them into one essence.' (Hauck – The Sorcerer's Stone).

In mythology, Hermes/Mercury was the messenger between the gods and mortals, instructing them from the realms of the Above to manifest in the Below. Mercury (Roman), Hermes (Greek), Thoth (Egypt) – all the same.

Chakras and Correspondences

Alchemists understood physical, energetic and mental life through understanding correspondences between the universe and the individual (also see chapter VIII). They forged links between planetary, physical and mental activity. They knew about Chakras – the energetic centres within the body – and their connection through the reflection of the solar system, in other words, astrological correspondence. The seven planets of our solar system relate to our psychological archetypes and physical organs which, in turn, correspond to particular herbs, oils and minerals. Alchemists also understood that the consciousness of the practitioner affected the outcome of a transformative process at a physical and molecular level centuries before it could be scientifically verified.

The Chakras reflect planetary principles in the areas and organs of the body where intelligence is located. The first and lowest (or 'root') chakra corresponds with Saturn, the largest planet. In the Indian yogic practice of Kundalini it is called *Muladhara.* It is the anchor, the earth-bound physicality of a body that deals with basic activity such as elimination. Lead is the mineral, a base metal from which the oil is extracted in the alchemist's laboratory. Raja Choudhury refers to chakras as a sacred map and to the esoteric concepts within Kundalini as being a Hermetic paradigm. In alchemical terms this is known as correspondence: the understanding that everything is *mind* and everything is a vibrating frequency of this mind; all mind that is everywhere is the same as each mind inside each body. The following chart clarifies the correspondences including those from Kundalini yoga practice.

The second Chakra is the sacral centre which matches Jupiter and water. This is the centre for reproduction, creativity, emotions and hormones.

The third Chakra is the digestive centre; here we not only digest food, but also the world, our 'reality' and our responses to it. Venus is the planet corresponding to the fourth Chakra which is the heart. This is the most powerful centre in terms of manifestation because it is responsible for feelings and feelings produce the electromagnetism that is the cause.

It is fifth dimensional and connects with the creative subconscious mind, fusing the left and right hemispheres of the brain. There is considerable

Element	Planet	Location	Chakra/Colour		Genre/Pitch/ Solfeggio	Attribute	Mineral
Cosmos	Sun	Crown	Sahasrara/ Violet	☉	Ragas/B/ 768–963hz	Awareness	Gold
Light	Moon	Brow	Ajna/Indigo	☽	Music of the Spheres/ Mozart/A/ 432–852hz	Perception	Silver
Ether	Mercury	Throat	Visuddha/Blue	☿	Opera/ high vocal/G/ 384–741hz	Expression	Mercury
Air	Venus	Heart	Anahata/ Green	♀	Choral/F/ 639hz	Empathy	Copper
Fire	Mars	Solar Plexus	Manipura/ Yellow	♂	Chanting/E/ 528hz	Will	Iron
Water	Jupiter	Lower Abdomen	Svadhisthana/ Orange	♃	Rock & Roll/ Latin/D/ 288–417hz	Creation	Tin
Earth	Saturn	Perineum	Muladhara/ Red	♄	Drumming/C/ 256–396 hz	Anchor	Lead

Figure 2

scientific evidence that the heart contains its own brain (cite Hagelin). The vortex of energy is far more powerful than the actual brain and the heart contains its own neutrons, protons and neurotransmitters enabling potentially rapid manifestation, healing and transformation. By activating this centre we realise that miracles are normal and constantly available to perform. And we are all performers.

The fifth Chakra is the throat and corresponds to Mercury which, as well as its planetary identity, is also the god of communication – the messenger. The throat houses the physical means of communication through speech, singing and oratory, and the oil of mercury is used in alchemical medicine as, indeed, all of the corresponding oils are. This fifth Chakra has an alchemical equivalent with the term Quintessence corresponding to ether and, just as the throat is the passage to the higher realms, ether is the transition from the physical elements to the non-physical. It appears in all spiritual traditions as the invisible energetic force that can be harnessed through practices such as Kundalini yoga, Tai Chi and Qigong. The throat is the gateway to the mind and spirit and the sixth Chakra which is the Brow centre, corresponding to the moon and to silver. This is also referred to as the third eye that looks within and 'watches the thinker' (Eckhart Tolle – *The Power of Now*). This shift to the world within leads to the Crown Chakra, the sun, the oil of gold and the spiritual realm. In both Kundalini yoga and in Buddhism the lotus flower is highly significant and replete with meaningful symbolism. There are specific numbers of petals associated with each chakra corresponding to the rising levels of consciousness or the ascension of Kundalini. The numbers are (starting from the root) 4, 6, 10, 12, 16, 2, 1000. The thousand petal lotus is the attainment of enlightenment. These energy centres do not end with the seventh chakra. The eighth is most significant because it is beyond the physical body and into the astral body and all that exists from there. The number eight is also highly symbolic in many spiritual practices for not dissimilar reasons – the gateway to the invisible world. It is always the beginning of a new level of spirituality. In his erudite book on *The Emerald Tablet,* Dennis W. Hauck writes:

> 'The Octad keeps recurring in our reality because it is a fundamental archetype on all levels of creation. Physically, psychologically and spiritually, the number eight drives the hidden processes of transformation. The secret

Eighth was a basic component of Hermetic doctrine since the beginning and has been openly incorporated into a number of esoteric disciplines...The octave is indeed the basic vibration of the whole universe, from the music of the spheres to the music that resonated below in human beings.... much of the phenomena around us can be interpreted in terms of the vibration of the seven tones of the musical scale.... The eighth step is a second beginning, sometimes even a Second Body, organized on a higher level (or Octave) that represents the fulfilment of what the previous seven steps had prepared.'

— (fn)

Sacred Numbers

Number sequences and the multiplicity of resulting patterns that form the physical world in myriads of repetitive and seemingly infinite symmetries and self-generating ratios are what is defined as sacred geometry. It is also sometimes referred to as organic mathematics and is evident everywhere and in everything from flowers to cathedrals, insects to snowflakes. The thinkers of ancient Egypt, Greece and India recognised that number sequences governed the physical world and believed that to study and understand their source would enable them to be closer to the Creator and to divinity. In his book *Sacred Geometry,* (cite) Robert Lawlor explains the system that determines the dimension and form of natural and man-made structures including the Golden Ratio, Fibonacci sequence, squaring the circle, and gnomonic expansion. He writes:

> 'Geometry is the study of *spatial order* through the measure and relationships of forms. Geometry and arithmetic, together with astronomy, the science of *temporal order* through the observation of cyclic movement, constituted the major intellectual disciplines

> of classical education. The fourth element of this great fourfold syllabus, the Quadrivium, was the study of harmony and music. The laws of simple harmonics were considered to be universals which defined the relationship and interchange between the temporal movements and events of the heavens and the spatial order and development on earth.'

To make this more accessible and to link it with chakras, minerals, Kundalini, and the human body we will consider the pine cone and the serpent. These two ancient symbols are connected and have been depicted in religions as diverse as Christianity and Kundalini Shakti. The pine cone is a geometrical manifestation of the Fibonacci number sequence which organically creates a logarithmic spiral. By its nature a spiral rises or falls depending on perception and the link with the serpent symbol is that of the rising and uncoiling of the snake/Kundalini which aims to reach the seventh Chakra, where the pineal gland resides, and thereby attain enlightenment, bliss and supreme consciousness. The serpent is energy which ascends the spinal cord to reach the knowledge residing in the pineal third eye. Serpents actually have a parietal eye on top of the head for the vision they are denied by being so low. The ancient Egyptians studied this eye as early as 3000 BC and their carvings can now be seen to represent a cross section of the brain – the pineal gland, the thalmus and the limbic brain area. They were the earliest spiritual scientists, cutting into the brain in an attempt to discover the source of knowledge. The rising serpent represents the reptilian brain which is responsible for survival, instinct and reaction. It is next to and a part of the limbic system responsible for emotions and knowledge. Then, *thirdly*, there is the neocortex which causes interference. The pineal (so called because it resembles a pine cone in its geometrical structure) *is* an eye with rods and cones. It produces melatonin (in the dark) causing sleep, and serotonin in the stomach, causing happiness. The pine cone and the serpent's head are inextricably linked, a clear example being the top of the Staff of Hermes which is depicted as a pine cone where the two serpents meet.

The pineal also produces DMT – dimethyltryptamine – which is a distortion of serotonin and is considered by many to be the gateway to the spiritual world. It creates extraordinary visions, creatures, psychic explosions and hallucinations which have transformed extreme rationalists into evangelical mystics, a recent and

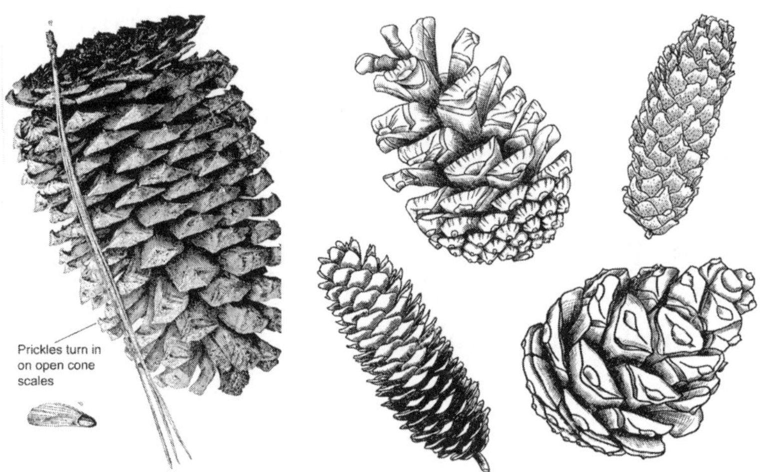

Figure 3

accessible example being Terence McKenna. Whatever the titles of his lectures, he invariably tangentialised into a talk on the impact of DMT. Dr. Rick Strassman writes about his research into the effects of DMT in his book *DMT – The Spirit Molecule* (Park Street Press 2001). In it he asserts that DMT, which is naturally released by the pineal gland, is the 'seat of the soul' and assists its transition in and out of the body. It is also the cause of encountering alien beings and abduction as well as profound mystical experiences and near death. He explors the potentially therapeutic, creative and spiritual use of psychedelics and the journey in crossing this largely unknown frontier that fuses science with consciousness. He describes his five year research project as the most remarkable and inspiring of his life, and his vision for future research and application is wholly uplifting and exciting.

All disciplines have asked (and still do ask) the same question, whether overtly or obliquely: can we activate the pineal gland at will? Michael Bradford writes:[1]

> 'The ultimate goal of this process is to enable a new faculty of perception – cosmic consciousness or enlightenment to function. When this faculty becomes fully operative it allows the individual to directly perceive consciousness as the primary reality.... Reality on the cosmic scale has a dual aspect – a static infinite Consciousness, designated as Shiva, and a dynamic creative power designated as Shakti. As an ancient Hermetic saying goes, "As Above, so Below". Thus, in the human body, the cosmic dynamic is paralleled by a centre of consciousness in the brain and a centre of creative power located in the base of the spine.'

---

1 Consciousness: The New Paradigm pub. ICR 2017

Signs and Symbols

Alchemy is known for its multitude of signs, symbols and secret codes. Some of the artwork is astonishingly detailed and colourful and the esoteric symbols abound both within the visual artefacts and also separately to signify a mineral, a process, a result or an idea. The reason for secrecy and coded information originates from the illegality of the practice in certain parts of the world, mainly the west, during the Dark Ages (476 C.E. – 1000 C.E.) when it stagnated to a large degree and was confined to Arabic countries. Later, after the invasion of Spain by Arabia, translations of their alchemical manuscripts and books spread rapidly through European countries and scholars tried to decipher the mysterious codes and symbols. Furthermore, even in the heyday of alchemy in Europe after 1200, and with the feverish excitement of translating the many texts and learning the art and science, those who acquired this extraordinary knowledge were reluctant to share it. They felt that it was not in their interest to inform the world how to transform lead into gold. To put it simply, having deciphered the various codes and signs, they continued to use them in their practice, thus perpetuating the esotericism. It is way beyond the scope of this book to explore the wealth of images and their significance, but there is an abundance of books on the subject, which, if nothing else, are beautiful to look at.

There are three symbols, however, that must be observed and explained at this point in order to grasp the concept of alchemy more clearly; they are the hexagram, the Caduceus, and the Philosopher's Stone. The hexagram is an ancient symbol traceable as far back as 3000 BC. It is loaded with a variety of meanings and powers that have been imposed on it by every faction of humanity both sacred and secular. It appears in every culture on earth and has been found on stone carvings, coins, buildings and various other artefacts from places and periods as diverse as fifth century BC Phoenicia, fourth century Bulgaria, on the plan for Stonehenge, on a coin of Herod the Great and on an Armenian Wheel of Eternity. It appears as a significant symbol in Buddhism, Hinduism, Islam and Judaism. It is fundamental to Freemasonry's esoterica, as it is to the Catholic Church's; the vestments within the Vatican are all embossed with it, including the Pope's hat. It is found on The Great Seal of the USA as well as appearing on Prince Albert's memorial in Hyde Park. In addition to all of this (and a great deal more), it's the Jewish Star of David, which has nothing to do with David;

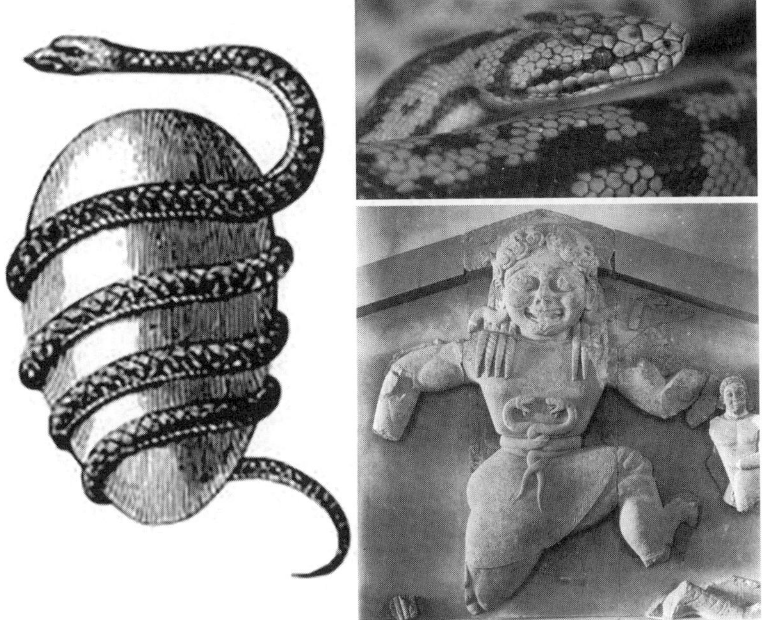

Figure 4

it was adopted when the Rothschilds appropriated it for the family crest, and they were neither Hebrew nor practising Jews – they simply funded the Zionist organisation when it adopted the hexagram in 1897. In Kundalini-Shakti it symbolises the union of opposites – yin/yang; Shiva/Shakti; male/female – which is where the alchemical relevance becomes apparent and the hexagram becomes significant.

In his book, *The Complete Idiot's Guide to Alchemy*, Dennis W. Hauck writes:

> 'Alchemy uses many opposing concepts, like Fire and Water, sun and moon, Mars and Venus, lead and gold, dryness and wetness, warmth and cold, volatile and fixed, matter and spirit. The union of these opposites constitutes a conjunction.'

The hexagram is a conjunction of two equilateral triangles. There is also an occult understanding of the numbers that produce the hexagon. By adding the three angles of sixty to equal 180, multiplied by two equals 360. Three sixes equals 666. Also by adding one up to thirty-six gives 666. In Freemasonry the symbol of intersecting compasses creates the same hexagon and above it is the Third Eye. Freemasonry is intricately bound up with alchemy, with Egypt and the pyramids which are also a reflection of the triangle. The pyramids were stairways to the divine; there is one on a dollar bill with the Third Eye at the top of it. From the Sumerians to the Egyptians, from Kabbalah to Catholicism, from Kundalini to Mayer Rothschild, the hexagon has been adopted and invested with supernatural and cosmic properties. It corresponds with Saturn (hence the various satanic references), and the north pole of the planet (which only receives sunlight every thirty years) is circled by a narrow jet stream travelling at 220 mph, forming a six sided hurricane sixty miles deep. Above it, another stream consisting of ammonia and hydrogen creates an aurora 'hovering' over the hurricane which *forms the shape of a hexagon.* This was discovered in the early '80s and observed again in 2009 when the sun returned.

The Caduceus is also known as The Staff of Hermes and is the symbol adopted by the medical profession. It also represents the Kundalini mechanism with the use of serpents to illustrate the awakening process which is common to almost all spiritual practices. Snakes and serpents have always represented rebirth and transformation together with fertility and the creative life-force. The Orouboros (a circular snake apparently swallowing its own tail) is another widely used symbol across many cultures to signify the cyclic nature of life and eternal renewal. The staff itself is the spinal cord around which two serpents are intertwined and meet at the top facing each other. This is the rising consciousness and the eventual balance between the two dualities (Shiva/Shakti, Yin/Yang, male/female) as they reach a higher state of awareness and balance and can soar towards enlightenment. Even the serpent in Genesis is a symbol for transformation. It is cast as evil, deceptive and cunning, but is actually the cause of a transformation in conscious awareness.

The Philosopher's Stone is the union of opposites. In alchemy this is referred to as The Great Work and is the product of The Sacred Marriage. The marriage between two substances is known as conjunction and can occur on a physical, mental, and spiritual level. At the level of Soul and Spirit it becomes Sacred and is considered to be the most vital aspect of inner transformation. This conjunction *within* inevitably manifests *without*, i.e. the body, the physical self, affecting attitude, behaviour and perception. This, in turn, affects relationships, decision making and life choices. Sleep space is also impacted and dreams gradually become more lucid. Anxiety disappears and is replaced by an inner calm and certainty which is non-reactive and quiet.

In the outer world the Stone has levels of manifestation, some more subtle than others and therefore harder to grasp. As a purely physical object, it is the result of transmuting lead into gold. But it is also much more than that. One can describe the physical properties of

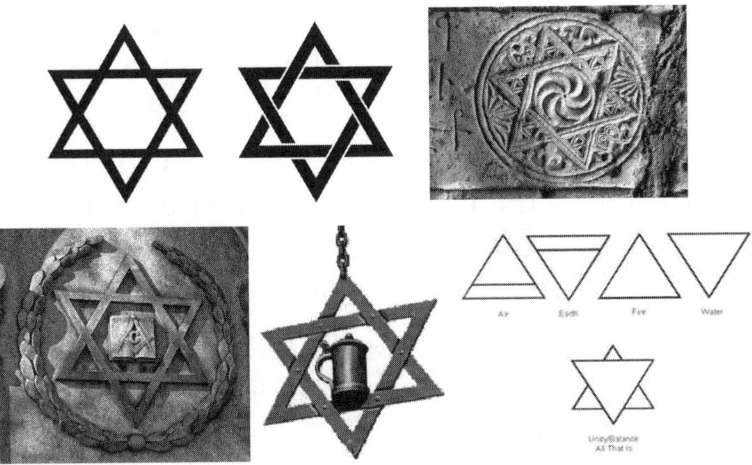

Figure 5

past Stones and what they looked like, how they came to exist and who was responsible. However, the essence of it lies in the relationship between consciousness and matter. It is *knowing* and *feeling* the truth of *The One Thing* in everything. It is experiencing the essential triune truth in all that constitutes the worlds within and without, Above and Below: Soul, Spirit, Body – Sulphur, Mercury, Salt. Gaze at a leaf, it is there; a star, a squirrel, a chair, a bus, your hand – they are all there. And when that is known, felt and truly experienced perception has shifted forever.

> 'Alchemy, magic, and modern science are slowly converging on the realization that

> mind is a force in nature and its purification and perfection are the Philosopher's Stone. Whether the perfection of consciousness is described as the magical touchstone of the alchemists, the power of focused attention of the magicians or the Grand Unified Theory of the physicists really does not matter. We are ultimately talking about the same thing – the power of mind or spirit over matter.'
>
> — Hauck: *The Complete Idiot's Guide to Alchemy.*

In terms of imagery, it proliferates in alchemic art, much of which includes two dragons with their necks twisted backwards as they reach for their opposing masculine and feminine forces to create balance and marriage, and they are seen to be balancing on the Stone. A more immediate and quasi scientific image which is referred to as 'squaring the circle' is of a circle (infinity) within which is a triangle (soul, spirit, body), within which is a square (earth, fire, air, water), within which is another circle and so on into infinity, thus representing the eternal and ultimately complete Philosopher's Stone.

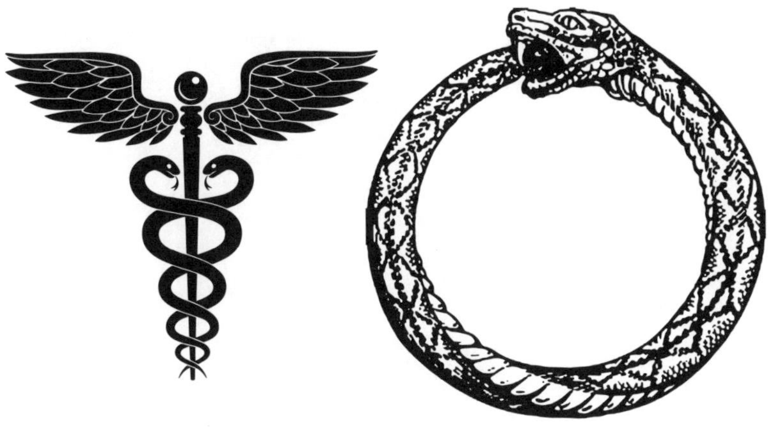

Figure 6

VI. The Alchemy of Performance

Alchemy is all about transformation. It can be defined as the relationship between consciousness and matter. In this chapter we will consider this relationship with regard to performance and, in particular, how we can use it to transform our experience.

The principal tenet of alchemy is, 'As above, so below; as within, so without.'

We will approach this truth at a purely psychological level as opposed to an operative or physical one. There is no need for us to explore the transformation of base metal into purer metals or scorpions into essential oil. However, these examples do represent the same principle exactly and a study of this science will certainly enhance and deepen the understanding of the psychological transformation with which we are concerned.

To begin, we will define performance in order to clarify our understanding and thereby liberate it from the many connotations associated with it. Performance: to act in fulfilment of a function. Further definitions arise from this, but this is the fundamental meaning.

The premise here is that we are almost always acting in fulfilment of a function and so by definition are in a *state* of performance far more than we perceive and are aware of. The tendency is to mentally and emotionally separate from everyday life the idea of performance as an unusual and demanding event that requires deliberate practice and attention, rather than a state that we occupy much of the time. It is this separation that can cause unwanted reactions and psychological obstacles and this is where transformation needs to take place if the actual musical (public) performance experience is to be free from anxiety and often debilitating physical symptoms as a consequence.

'As within, so without.'

The alchemy of performance lies in the psychological transformation whereby our perceptions are altered, which in turn changes our experience. This is achieved by conscious use of the imagination (chapter

2). Performance anxiety is entirely psychological. It is our psychological state that causes emotional and physical reactions. This can lead to a 'cycle of fear', whereby the anxiety causes an emotional response, which causes physical symptoms, which exacerbate the anxiety and increase the power of the cycle. All of this starts 'within'. Furthermore, if we examine, as we must, the cause of the anxiety in the first instance, it is fear of the (imaginary) 'without'. And it is fictional, as are most 'withouts'.

The Alchemical Process

The process of transformation in alchemy operates over three distinct phases. These are colour-coded to correspond with the base metal's development from black through white to red.

Each of these material phases has a corresponding psychological one and the transformation spanning seven distinct applications and tasks can and should be understood both within and without. Each affects the other and medieval alchemists knew this. They knew that the state of consciousness of the scientist influenced the outcome. This is fundamentally the same as the law of attraction, of manifestation, of co-creation. Six hundred years later, society is slowly grasping the truth and power of this law, mainly because science can measure and prove it through quantum physics. Carl Jung, one of the most influential psychotherapists of the twentieth century, was also an alchemist and knew that the two are inseparable. He knew that if one wanted to alter circumstances the process must begin in the mind.

The Three Phases

The Black Phase: Negredo

Calcination
Dissolution

The White Phase: Albedo

Separation
Conjunction

The Red Phase: Rubedo

Fermentation
Distillation
Coagulation

There follows a list of correspondences between the within and the without to clarify the inherent union and relationship between consciousness and matter.

Negredo – The Black Phase

Calcination

Within	**Without**
Personal	Physical
Getting rid of the false ego; burning bad habits and mental artifice.	Heating a substance in an open flame, or using acids.

Dissolution

The subconscious = the unknown 'shadow' self, storing negative beliefs that need to dissolve. Depression.	Dissolving the ashes from calcination in a liquid which then takes on magical qualities.

Albedo – The White Phase

Separation

To rediscover and isolate your true self and protect it from egotistical contamination.	Extracting and preserving the pure essences from the contaminated that were revealed in dissolution.

Conjunction

Growth of spiritual fetus, personal stone.	Recombination of purified essences into a new compound.

Rubedo – The Red Phase

Fermentation

Acceptance of spiritual power. Inspiration. Higher form of imagination, of spiritual reality.	Conversion of organic substance into new compounds with fermenting bacteria.

Distillation

Deliberate pursuit of insight through conscious reconciliation of subjective and objective experience, in order to refine the psychic state.	Heat and condense a solution to intensify its concentration. Rectification is the repetition of this process.

Coagulation

The healed person. Awareness beyond gender. Liberation, nirvana. Phoenix. Inner reality recognised.	Philosopher's Stone: spiritual > physical; physical > spiritual. Manifestation created, born and purified. Transmutation.

Alchemy is a conscious and deliberate procedure as described here. The key to understanding it, however, is to see that it also operates unconsciously to varying degrees. It is both art and science. It is a truth. As humans we possess the instinct to grow, develop, transform, improve, expand, learn. Growth is inevitable and unavoidable throughout the universe, which is constantly expanding. Alchemy applies the truth of transformation to all substance including thought, psychological states and emotional states. It recognises and activates the immense power generated by the art/science of manifestation and transmutation.

Everyone has a choice regarding their level of consciousness and one's state of mind is the only real possession possible for sentient beings. What alchemists knew even 600 years ago is that a state of mind (level of consciousness) creates the phenomenal world, because that's what the phenomenal world is.

> As above, so below.
>
> As within, so without.

They knew the law of metaphysics.

Performance

Performance is a psychological state and one that we occupy by default much of the time. Most people manage this condition reasonably well, but there are those who do not, and their numbers are increasing. There are several reasons for this. One is that there are, simply, more people. Another is that there is relatively less live interaction and more virtual interaction. The soaring growth of clinically diagnosed anxiety in university students has to be a testament to their sense of isolation and consequent fear when in a social/group environment, which they inevitably must be. Many of them are overwhelmed by their awareness of the act of performance when they have to enter a room of people, speak in a seminar or contribute in any form of interactive workshop. And this is true across all disciplines.

The fundamental premise of this book is this: if we want to change our experience in performance, the process of transformation needs to begin a long time before the event and to be addressed as constantly as attention will allow.

This is because what is undergoing transformation is consciousness. The alchemy of performance is the transmutation of levels of consciousness from the psychological equivalent of lead into gold. Lead is asleep. Gold is enlightened. 'Gold thinking' doesn't know about performance nerves, anxiety or fear because they don't exist.

How to achieve Transformation

The first step is to acknowledge that performance is a psychological state and a state is something that we occupy – sometimes by choice but more often by default. It is not possible to not occupy a state because it is impossible to stop thinking. Therefore, it is with our thoughts that the work begins (in alchemy it is known as The Great Work).

The chaotic and ramshackle nature of most of our thinking is the cause (prima materia – black earth) of all suffering. When someone suffers from anxiety about a forthcoming event (an interview, audition, public speech, wedding etc), the source is their thoughts – and only their thoughts. We are afraid of our psychological state because of the emotion that will result and in turn how it will make us feel. This entire experience is *within*. Common practice is to fantasise and even assume that the various (fictitious) causes are without – people, environment, the 'unknown' – but it can't be any of those things. And our anxiety levels will remain, irrespective of the extent to which we have control over any or all of the external circumstances.

Therefore, it is the within that must be addressed, as is always the case. Every event that occurs in the external world is essentially neutral. It can't be anything else; it's an event. The interpretation of it which causes emotional, psychological and intellectual responses, is what defines it as a disaster, a victory, a loss or a gain, a happy event or a cause for concern. Any one event can *affect* all of these reactions and more, but it is not the *cause*. The cause is the variety of states that are responding.

Imagine your 'world within' to be a house – a mansion even – which has been ransacked and left in complete chaos. It is so bad that it is hard to even identify the function of the various rooms. It is also extremely noisy as radios have been left playing all over the house, each tuned to a different station. Where does one start? It feels impossible. But it only feels that way because you've chosen to turn around (inward), look at it and hear it. You've been tolerating it for years, perhaps not always with ease, but mostly managing to muddle through. There are those who simply cannot stand it and, not knowing how to cope, imbibe some substance to escape and feel release. Addicts are usually closer to awareness than they are given credit for; because they cannot attain the consciousness they unknowingly crave, they opt for oblivion. They can't put up with the noise and mess.

Negredo – The Black Phase

The first step is a huge one, but in the act of turning round and facing *it,* the journey has begun. This is **Negredo** and it is tempting to (psychologically) torch the whole thing. It is painful, humbling, and can cause feelings of shame, guilt, unworthiness and even depression. Of course no-one wants this experience, but the burning and destruction of the very cause of all anxiety is the only path to liberation.

Most people need assistance with this, obviously, and guidance comes in many forms. The initial task, however, is totally the responsibility of each individual and requires the exploration and examination of one's internal landscape – the world within. This requires deliberate, conscious thought and attention. It is both simple and extremely difficult. The difficulty lies in paying attention.

By the time we are eighteen we are already riddled with habits, both physical and psychological. Changing physical habits is known to be challenging, especially with any addictive behaviour. But our mental habits are also highly addictive and frequently toxic. They are the cause of our feelings of anxiety, fear, unworthiness and self-doubt. That is why they have to go; they have to be 'burned', which cannot happen unless they are acknowledged, faced and felt. On a purely practical level this means noticing, listening and remembering to do both. You are listening to the constant conversation going on in your head. What are you saying – to yourself, to others, about others? How do you react to people, events and circumstances? It is vital to become aware, to become conscious of the world within in a deliberate, objective and non-critical manner. If you attack yourself for the paucity of your habitual thinking you merely perpetuate the very cause you're attempting to 'burn', i.e. rid yourself of.

Notice dispassionately the condition of your internal landscape and make this a new habit. The first step is to notice, listen as often as your attention will allow. Practise and repeat, practise and repeat. Calcination is the hardest part by far and takes the longest, so the consolation is that the only way is up.

The second stage of **Negredo** is called dissolution and is governed by water, which is necessary after the fires of calcination. It involves the liquidation of solid into fluid. Having acknowledged and burned the psychological habits and egotistical mental structures during calcination, it is then necessary to dissolve the remains – the ashes. This can cause distress, sadness, crying and even depression, but it is a natural and necessary process which is ultimately very liberating. One experiences a type of death: the death of an old familiar self, of lifelong habits, perspectives and reactions, which can feel like loss on a grand scale. Although the goal is to grow beyond these states, there can be resistance to releasing the familiar. It also involves re-experiencing past pain, 'facing one's demons', releasing old anger, tears, fears that have been trapped in the subconscious for decades causing varying degrees of mental and emotional suffocating. The potential energy released from this process can be truly life-altering – which is, after all, the point.

Albedo – The White Phase

At the darkest and lowest point of Negredo (the previous phase), when one can feel quite lost, the beginning of recovery and growth appear. The two processes are known as separation and conjunction. In the laboratory this is the separation of whatever substances have survived Negredo from the detritus that has not. The skill of the alchemist is to keep them apart and avoid contamination. If this part fails, the entire experiment also fails. Psychologically, after the misery of Negredo and the personal death undergone, we recognise a cleaner, purer, 'whiter' essence of ourselves. This integral self is the true nature and must be preserved and kept away from all that was dispensed with in Negredo. It is critical to be highly attentive during this phase because the experience of dissolution is relatively recent, and the new sense of self is not yet a secure habit, which means that we are vulnerable and that contamination is still possible.

Having to continue with domestic and professional life is enormously challenging to a newly born and fragile sense of self. It is still easy for attention to sway and to be drawn to old patterns. It will be as it was before, but it is vital to always be in contact with one's inner world to some degree in the phase of separation.

Conjunction

The White Phase of separation leads directly into that of conjunction, which is where most failures occur. It is the process of recombining the surviving essences into a (lesser stone) of united duality. This is a spiritual science. It is not a belief system, but scientific fact. And it isn't new because truth cannot be new – it just is. It is the unification of soul and spirit, whether in solid matter or in psychological experience. In the laboratory it is the recombination of the saved elements into a new, separated and finer compound. This result isn't inevitable however. It is possible to put two or more elements into the two glass globes, which then do not form a compound when they meet in the connecting tube, but remain separate. The reasons for this can be contamination (impurities), pollution through negative vibration, and, most interestingly, the consciousness of the practitioner.

Alchemy has been defined as the relationship between consciousness and matter. Human beings are able to affect substance with their psychological and emotional state. This is a truth. The only development of this truth is that it can now be measured by scientists (quantum physicists).

At a personal level it is the union of male and female, thought and feeling, soul and spirit, thereby creating a higher state that is able to intuit and experience life from a newly insightful perspective. The reason for possible failure is described above; this new 'child' is not able to cope with the world of stressful demands and so it essentially dies – that is, the possibility of your alchemically transformed self dies, which is a huge setback.

Conjunction is the crucial pivot in the alchemical process. It is the transition from the Below to the Above. The next phase, Rubedo, deals with the realms of spirit, vibration and energy.

Rubedo – The Red Phase

The Red Phase is the beginning of the work Above, the work Below having been completed at the close of Albedo. The work Above is concerned with energy, spirit and a higher consciousness. After graduating from Rubedo, the initiated being then reflects the new enlightenment/insight/transformation onto the Below, which was the motive for the entire process: how to enhance and develop one's performance in all areas of life.

The processes during Rubedo are fermentation, distillation and coagulation. Fermentation is a natural process that occurs when organic matter is allowed to rot and decay and the bacteria that grow convert the substance into a new compound. Additional substances can be added to produce a particular result, the most well-known being wine, beer and spirits. Alchemists considered alcohol to be the spiritual essence of a substance, hence the term 'spirits'.

When matter is left to rot and decompose in the first stage of fermentation it is known as putrefaction. There is a darkness to this stage, but not that experienced in Negredo, because the process state is much more advanced. It is the necessary shadow of decay that produces the fermenting bacteria that has the connotation of death and destruction, but which is temporary and will actually give birth to a greater and brighter life.

At a chemical level this can be whiskey, wine, beer etc, all of which are revolting in the early stages of their growth, but which produce a glorious, bright, life-enhancing substance.

At a personal level this is the transition to a heightened awareness of the world within. It is the beginning of the realisation that there is only ever one cause and this becomes stronger as we move through distillation to coagulation. Our sense of personal power increases in a non-egotistical way and we experience inspiration, stronger intuition and a gravitation towards spiritual development. At this level we may be attracted to therapeutic classes – yoga, tai chi, meditation groups etc – because of the energetic and excited psychic motivation felt. For that reason it is at this early stage that we have to be highly discerning.

Distillation

This is the reduction of a liquid to increase its concentration. There are several methods, but the most common is to boil and reduce (or, in the case of a sauce, simmer and reduce until the desired intensity is reached) or to repeatedly boil and condense to increase the purity and intensity of the vapours.

Alchemists treasured the pure spirit of alcohol, and any whiskey, gin or vodka distillery will impart the same sentiment.

Personal distillation actually occurs to varying degrees by default, in that there is a general tendency for self-improvement. Most people have a desire to be kinder, more compassionate, empathetic etc, with chaotic and sporadic attempts at refining their thinking. Slow, inconsistent progress might be made.

Deliberate personal distillation is a completely different matter. It requires application, concentration and repetition. Old habits die hard and we must be vigilant at this stage to ensure that no past impurities creep back into the newly liberated and purified self. Humans are repetitive by nature, both mentally and physically. We think the same thoughts almost cyclically, even though we dislike most of them, and our emotional reactions are wholly predictable because we have felt them countless times, even though we also dislike many of them.

It is clear, therefore, that unconscious repetition must be met with intensely conscious and purposeful repetition. No matter how thoroughly we may grasp an insight, a truth, an idea or a fact, it will not change our minds on one or even several readings. We have to continually repeat the input in whatever form (written, aural) until our subconscious mind has accepted it as factual truth. This means that we feel it and it has become who we are.

Just as the alchemists can distil a substance many times over to increase its purity and concentration, so we must repeatedly distil any residual impurities from an inflated ego to a deflated one, so that there is no further risk of the shadows of anxiety, fear, doubt or sense of inadequacy, because the last traces of them have gone forever.

Coagulation

This is the final stage in the alchemical process of transformation and the language with which to describe it needs to be carefully chosen. Anyone who even takes an interest in the alchemical trajectory must be looking for some sense of liberation and growth. There is not a religion in the world for which this is not true. While alchemy is not a religion, it is a truth.

The truth is that the world within creates the world without. Therefore, the world without reflects the world within.

Imagination is the creator of the world; it is the one thinking substance from which and by which all things are made. We all have imagination but it is mostly skidding like mercury across a hot surface (such a wonderful alchemical metaphor).

Coagulation is a harnessing of the limitless power of imagination and awakening to the potential for personal control over creation. This immediately liberates you from competition and rivalry which in turn release anxiety and doubt. The competitive mind is not the creative mind. Anxiety and fear cannot survive in the truly creative and conscious mind.

Coagulation is when we emerge as the new self – liberated, conscious and powerful within. The body becomes aware of its spirituality and the spirit of its physical manifestation. As within, so without; as without, so within. Above, below; below, above.

The Phoenix is the symbol most often associated with coagulation. In mythology it rose from the ashes as a resurrected and newly born creature. Other symbols include an egg (birth), androgynous youth, scales (balance) and various images of opposites joining and becoming complete.

Paracelsus wrote:

> 'It is the completely healed human being who has burned away all the dross of his lower being and is free to fly as the Phoenix.'
>
> — Dennis Hauck – *The Complete Idiot's Guide to Alchemy.*

The alchemical process is the path to realising the great truth that sets you free: that everything in your world is a manifestation of the mental activity that goes on within you, and that the conditions and circumstances of your life only reflect the state of consciousness with which you are fused.

To fully inhabit this truth requires concentrated, deliberate and repetitive application. Concentration should be intense interest, which always produces positive results. There is no more worthwhile use of time than changing one's mind. It is the end of suffering.

VII. The Wisdom of Repetition

Writers and thinkers over centuries have been expounding the truth about our existence. There is not a single original revelation in this book. The reason for creating it, as with so much of this type of writing, is to bring seemingly disparate threads of perception together in order to emphasise the underlying messages that we all share, and to focus attention on applying them to the practical business of performance, with all that it entails.

This is the starting point for the wisdom of repetition:

1. Alchemy as an ancient art and science. It separates and unites. Over centuries of apparent development art and science have been separated as disciplines and have influenced education enormously as a result. We are currently experiencing a re-unification, not only of art and science, but

of an increasing number of areas of human existence that have formerly been considered mutually exclusive, such as science as spirituality.

2. The cyclic repetition of birth, growth, decay, and death. The ever decreasing cycles of repetition within the larger: seasons, months, weeks, days, hours, and minutes. The repetitive movement of planets which provide the cyclic rhythms that we live by, within and without, above and below.
3. And then, from the patterns of the universe, the reflection of those patterns in the individual organism of a human being. Every cell, neutron, photon, is a universe, is the universe. In the past 30 years, science has been able to measure and therefore prove what Eastern philosophers have always known.

'Liberation while living is considered in Indian life to be the highest experience – a fusion of the individual with the universal ... The human organism, the microcosm, parallels everything in the macrocosm. The complete drama of the universe is repeated here, in this very body. The whole body with its biological and psychological processes becomes an instrument through which the cosmic power reveals itself.'

— Kundalini, *The Arousal of the Inner Energy*, Ajit Mookerjee, 1982, Thames & Hudson

'[Nichiren Daishonin] taught that our existence is identical to the universe as a whole, and the universe as a whole is identical to our existence. Each individual human life is a microcosm of the life of the universe.'

— Nichiren Buddhism (See appendix 1).

We are made of repetition, of patterns, rhythms, and cycles at every level – cellular, psychological, and spiritual.

The repetition of thought is both necessary and self-defeating depending on use, concentration and, above all, consciousness. We can use our thoughts to create or destroy, or simply allow some nebulous state in between, which may achieve either or both, but which doesn't deliberately create for the purpose of growth, expansion, and awareness. The default is mostly habitual and often negative repetition of almost

Tourette-like thought, most of which is abysmally lazy, tired, and formless.

When we deliberately programme our brain with clear intention for a desired outcome, we do so most efficiently through the conscious application of repetition. The best of repetition is capable of anything – the 'mustard seed that can move mountains' (Matthew 17.20). The worst of it can be a type of living death; it is actively damaging and destructive. Much of humanity is unaware that there is a choice, but the truth and the knowledge of it has always been. In performance, our default repetitive thoughts intensify considerably and we are in no position to do any reprogramming. Even when we know how senseless and counterproductive they are we remain powerless to arrest the flow and this lack of control increases the anxiety. This is the strength of repetition at its worst, running wildly on past data. Every nerve-racking performance adds to the belief system that created the anxiety initially. There are many gifted musicians and artists who stop performing because of their inability to break these debilitating cycles of self-sabotaging thoughts. The sad irony is that they possess the very attributes needed to overcome them far more than many people do. To become an accomplished musician requires years of rigorous repetitive application and thought in order to establish technical control, sensitive and informed musicianship with expression and interpretation. If these skills were applied to the world within, the entire inner landscape could be familiar, peaceful and wholly benign; and so, therefore, would the audience.

There needs to be a specific process in order to achieve a transfer of a specialised skill set from one highly recognisable trajectory to what might feel to be foreign territory. Just as many musicians and artists of all disciplines have a daily routine, a practice schedule and a goal plan (often the practical one of a deadline/concert etc.), a lasting shift in perception requires at least as much attention. The adoption of new thought patterns and reduction of habitual reactions requires spending allocated time every day on short and simple activities without opinion, resistance or judgement. It can be entirely mechanical at first and, for some, bewildering (usually those who need it most). None of it is difficult, strenuous or physically painful. Appendix 5 is a suggested list with which to get started. I have never known it to fail when consistently applied. It includes such things as writing a gratitude list, short meditation, being outdoors and aware of nature and, above all, observation – not demanding, but highly effective. Gradually, what happens is the musical discipline of committed regularity regardless of whimsical distraction, which has served to facilitate this new inner practice, in turn benefits enormously – as do all other areas of one's life.

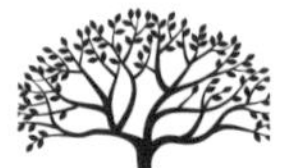

Neville Goddard (1905 – 1972) wrote extensively on what he considered to be the most misunderstood book in the world – The Bible. In his book, *The Creative Use of Imagination*, he writes:

> 'The Bible, the most wonderful book in the world and the most misunderstood, is your personal autobiography. It is not the recording of historical events as your teachers teach, and its writings were never intended to be interpreted as such ... The Bible is speaking of the heaven within and the earth without. Its story begins: "In the beginning God created heaven and earth. And the earth was without form and a void; and the darkness was upon the face of the deep. Then the spirit of God said, 'Let there be light,' and there was light."

> 'The light spoken of here comes from the heaven which is within you... It is your consciousness. The outer man (called the earth) is dark, while the inner man (called heaven) is the being who was in the beginning with God and was God, but is sound asleep. As your autobiography, the Bible tells you how you are lifted up from your present level of being into a higher one.'

Of the Gospels, he wrote:

> 'These writings give four biographical sketches of a principle rather than a man. It took 900 years for the Bible to come into its present form. So, when you read it, always bear in mind that it is speaking of the Kingdom of Heaven within you ... All that is recorded in scripture are aspects of your mind.'

As an example of repetitive writing and lecturing, Neville Goddard must be unsurpassed. The core of his message could probably be condensed to fewer than 4,000 words (minus examples and case studies), and yet he has produced ten books and delivered countless lectures, all on the same subject (because he has only one subject): the power of the imagination to manifest the desired state and experience.

It has been said that if one truly understood one sentence from *A Course In Miracles* (citation), the essence of the entire text would be understood also. This is the power and necessity of repetition. When a shift in perception is required to grasp a 'new' principle or concept, it has to be repeated constantly for a lasting change to occur. Alteration of perception means to change one's mind, which is easier said than done. It requires repetitive, conscious practice to change anything with lasting psychological and valued emotional benefits, whether it be playing a musical instrument, public speaking, waterskiing, tight-rope walking, chess, ballet dancing or Formula 1. At a level of mind, it is all the same.

So many of our thoughts and beliefs aren't actually our own. Throughout childhood we absorb the opinions and perspectives of others, which, together with our experiences, form an internal blueprint through which we filter these beliefs in order to understand and interpret them so as to form a programme by which we live and react and develop what we assume to be our own opinions and belief systems, but which really belong to other people (many more than we might imagine). This forms our automatic responses and reactions and, therefore, our experience of 'the world'.

The subconscious mind is programmed from birth; it is utterly obedient and highly resistant to change. It will slavishly fulfil our concept of ourselves, thereby perpetuating the very life situation that we may wish to improve. Until it is understood that lasting change is not possible until the subconscious mind has been addressed, circumstances will continue to repeat themselves. Even when people experience a large lottery win, more often than not, the winners' life situations revert to normal within a relatively short time. It has been said often that if the world's wealth was evenly distributed, the gross imbalance would eventually revert back to the original model because of the attitudes, motivations, and beliefs of the population. Evidence of this abounds just within the narrow perspective of lottery fortune. Michael Carroll became a minor celebrity in 2002 after he had won £9.7 million which he managed to squander in eighteen months, including an investment of £1 million into Glasgow Rangers and an alcohol and cocaine habit that contributed to a substantial jail sentence. Evelyn Adams gambled her £5.4 million and ended up living in a trailer. Luke Pittard, having experienced the lavish holiday, wedding and home, grew bored and returned to work in McDonald's. Stories like these are the norm.

The conscious mind is slow. The subconscious mind works at lightning speed and it is the subconscious mind that is in control, much as we like to believe otherwise. It is always several moves ahead of the conscious mind and, unless it has been deliberately and repeatedly reprogrammed, it will be acting on those old programmes that are mostly installed by others. Not all of them are negative or detrimental to well-being, but those that are govern growth rate, progress, and happiness.

Clearly, what is required is the reprogramming of the subconscious mind where necessary, and the first step is to identify those beliefs that are obstacles to anything you might wish to achieve. This requires bypassing the conscious mind to some degree in order to identify the programmes that are being held. The subconscious mind and the physical body have their own relationship and are able to communicate directly without interference from the thinking, opinionated mind. This can enable identification of held programmes. For example, there is the thumb test as described by Uwe Albrecht in his book *YES/ NO – arm length testing for instant answers and well-being.* If a decision has to be made – it could be about which wine to buy or who to marry – hands are placed behind the back and the question is asked. The hands are then brought to the front with the thumbs together. If they're level, it's 'yes'; if not, it's 'no'. This and other arm-length tests are described and explained in his book (Hay House 2012).

Another instant example is the sway test. Stand straight, feet together pointing forward and feel balanced. Say something to yourself that is obviously untrue, such as 'I live in India'. You will sway backwards. Then try, 'I'd love more money' and see what happens. Unless you're a Russian oligarch, you'll probably tilt forward. With this information put to creative and manipulative use, it's possible to identify and therefore alter all that is determining your experience.

During the first five to seven years of our lives, our brains are mostly harmoniously balanced and behaving like sponges, absorbing *everything*. This is our left and right hemispheres talking to each other and allowing playful absorption of all that occurs. We have not yet learned, but are gradually learning, emotional and psychological resistance.

As adults, the most efficient way to systematically reprogramme the subconscious mind is to replicate the mental state of a child in order to replace old, fake programmes with ones that have been chosen. The conscious mind cannot do this. You could read this book once, believe every word, feel that your life has been altered – and absolutely nothing will change. Unless you address and know how to treat and make use of the subconscious mind, nothing ever will. You cannot reprogramme by reading a book or attending a lecture. These are for inspiration. You can only create real change by repetition – for as long as it takes. Furthermore, this application of repetition is most effective when the brain is relaxed and balanced. This can also be achieved in meditation, which is arguably the most effective and controllable method that exists, but it isn't the only one. There are innumerable YouTube channels playing hours of 'brainsync' binaural beats to lull one into a theta state with the promise of inducing innumerable benefits both psychological and material. While they won't cause any damage, and may even promote relaxation and sleep, they are not meditation. (See Appendix 2 for meditation techniques.) Meditation is based on repetition – repetition of a mantra, an intention, a mental rhythm, in order to bring oneself into an observational state of being and stillness which becomes unassailable.

VII. The Wisdom of Repetition

From the mid 1950s through to the late 1970s a new musical genre developed and flourished, first in California then migrating to New York. It was and is known as Minimalism and is based on the transcendental powers of repetition. At its core was the idea of long held notes, the harmony from which changed so slowly that an intentional sense of timeless stillness arose which was hypnotic, meditative, and spiritual. The observation of the very gradual harmonic transformation was achieved through lengthy repetitive sequences that acted as drones to create a wholly non narrative, non linear experience resulting from the manipulation of time itself. John Cage (of whom more in the following chapter) was the forerunner of the minimalist movement and prepared the site for these composers by providing them with the freedom to challenge the past in an iconoclastic fashion. After having declared that Beethoven was completely misguided (which Cage did), the way was fairly clear for further experiment and challenging well established norms. In California, the two composers who began what was to become the most successful subgenre of classical music were Terry Riley and LeMont Young, both of whom are still alive and composing. They both studied Indian classical music for around thirty years and actually became disciples of Pandit Pran Nath in order to study Ragas, a form of music designed to affect the mind and alter the emotional condition of the listener. They are also built on drones and are composed for their vibrational alignment with the unseen world and to reflect the cyclic nature of the universe. They embrace a far greater timescale and concept than that of the linear, narrative and structural approach of western composition, whether in the classicism of the eighteenth and nineteenth centuries or the serialism and polytonality of the twentieth. Riley and Young also learned that the consciousness (presence) of the composer was able to impact the vibrational nature of the Ragas, many of which were written for certain times of the day in order to heighten the awareness of the listener. Indeed, recordings of Ragas are frequently played in empty rooms in the belief that the vibrational space will be enhanced.

All of this has a colossal impact on western music because it crossed the hitherto clear threshold between classical and popular identities and for a long time it was unclassifiable. This was highly positive for several reasons, the main one being that of inclusion. Whether of performers, audiences, listeners, and even non-active listeners, it created a musical democracy (particularly for performers) in which everyone had a part to play and a contribution to make. Not only was it the hybrid between classical and popular music, it promoted involvement at every level and aimed to close the chasm between performer and audience. This in turn greatly reduced the anxiety levels of performers because of the sense of everyone being involved. As Cage said, the music is completed by the listener. This is not to say that anxiety was completely absent, but it was of a quite different nature. It could almost be described as 'positive' and the opposite of the personal, self-absorbed fear of isolated exposure. The concentration required in whatever capacity one is involved leaves no room for that! The immersive quality of the performance *because of the repetition, inclusion and shared responsibility* affords all participants (i.e. everyone) a feeling of selfless, joyful contribution. Which is what we all love.

Minimalism was a fusion of repetition, transcendence and technology. It was made possible because of tape (initially) and then from the rapid growth in the ability to reproduce sound.

When it 'moved' to New York and was developed so inexorably by Philip Glass and Steve Reich, it changed the perception of serious music for the western world and it continues to embrace people rather than exclude them. 'New Music Societies' (universities and other) tend to encourage all newcomers. No auditions, but a belief that everyone has something valuable to give. There is a strong tendency to blame technology for our attention deficit and short concentration spans, but resistance and nostalgia are stagnant. Brains function differently now and we must embrace them by using the apparent cause to facilitate an effect that can advance our consciousness rather than deplete it.

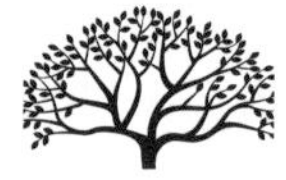

In his extensive course entitled *Mastering Alchemy,* Jim Self explains the shift in dimensional reality from the third through the fourth to the fifth (dimensions). He aligns the fifth dimension in particular to the solar cycles from 400 years to eleven years. He explains the impact that these cycles, together with the sun's magnetism, has had and is currently having on human beings through the electrical nature of thought and the magnetic nature of emotion. He states that the earth's magnetic field is decreasing and that between 2000 and 2010 it did so by ten per cent, followed by almost another ten per cent from 2010 to 2017. He estimates that by 2035 it will have reduced by fifty per cent. We are electrical and magnetic beings who are mostly oblivious to the effect that the solar cycles and subsequent activity have on our psyches. '(In 2012) the shift came, the transition from 3rd to 4th dimension started. It impacted all things, especially human beings, the experience being one of instability, increased anxiety, feelings of fraudulence and inadequacy.' (Jim Self – Webinar).

He also explains the way in which it is an alchemical process in that it is transformative through higher levels of consciousness. The third dimension functions on the linear concept of time, which is applied rather than fixed. There is past, present, future and death. Our future is largely based on past messages and beliefs. There is also reaction, which repeatedly manifests itself and is mostly caused by our unsatisfactory concept of ourselves and the way we imagine we are seen and perceivedby others.

Many of us are in varying states of anticipation, worry and defence, all of which amount to a level of fear – the blight of this dimension that almost defines it. It is both global and personal, because they are reflective. In the fourth dimension, we begin to experience choice and present time. To whatever degree we imagine that these already exist, the difference is palpable when reaction is removed. Reaction is emotional and draining, and is the third dimension's way of life. It causes conflict, stress, mood swing, and damage. It is a superficial response born of ignorance. Fourth dimensional consciousness ceases to dwell in the past, having chosen to focus on the present. Most people do their best in any situation, even supposedly disastrous parents, teachers, priests. No-one willingly chooses to injure or inflict suffering; it's done for a motive that is mostly unconscious. The phrase, 'there but for the grace of god' refers to the insight that if we had experienced the same history as the one being condemned, we would be the condemned. Fourth dimensional thinking and feeling retreats from critical judgement and appreciates a broader picture in which we all exist. Through it, the truth that 'there is only one of us here' can be perceived, as can the Moses code, 'I am that I am'.

Fourth dimensional consciousness ceases to allow the past to hold it hostage – either our own past or anyone else's to which we may have 'fallen victim'.

It becomes irrelevant and even dull, dispensed with, rather like finally putting down an extremely heavy backpack that is no longer needed (and never was) – a huge relief.

The fourth dimension is one of choice and observance (if and how to react) and a keener insight into what actually matters. It creates calm, serenity, well-being, peace, and effortless control. It is a thought realm.

In the fifth dimension, we become conscious of being unconscious, and then conscious of being conscious. There is an abiding sense of calm and well-being unaffected by circumstance; non-reactive but observant and not emotionally involved at a self-impacting level. Aware of being aware, in the world, but not of it, we have the capacity to dismantle the insanity of third dimensional existence with insight, compassion and empathy.

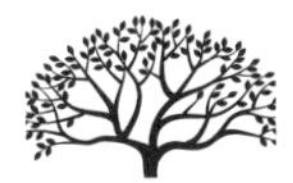

Lucie Green is a solar scientist who works at the Mullard Space Science Laboratory of UCL. She is particularly interested in Coronal Mass Ejections and the ways in which they are caused by the sun's magnetic field. A CME releases vast amounts of electromagnetic radiation and matter made up of protons and electrons, forming a magnetised plasma. These can produce solar flares and sunspots, which are caused by the flares forming groups. Sunspots appear in magnetically polarised pairs that appear as darker spheres on the sun's surface. The rearrangement of magnetic field lines release energy that is stored within them. It becomes increasingly twisted, tightened and stressed so that the CME acts as a trigger to eject and release it.

In 1859, the Carrington Event was an enormous CME – a solar superstorm which, if it occurred today, would result in the loss of ten per cent of our satellite fleet, with huge consequences for weather forecasting, military services, and electrical transmission work.

The sun is an electrically charged spherical ball of fluid. Consequently, its violent, dynamic, unstable and constantly changing magnetic field threads through it and absorbs energy that can be unleashed to power a CME.

Solar cycles affect us whether they occur in 400 years, eleven years or anywhere in between. In 2012 there was a dramatic shift in the solar cycle, which, although it could have been far more violent, nonetheless had a significant impact on our planet. There was a near miss from a CME geomagnetic storm. In July of that year, the sun produced a series of rapid CMEs which were ejected from the 'side' of the sun (to us), therefore not aimed at earth. The magnetic field and particle density information were measured and from that data it was concluded that, had it erupted from a different aspect of the sun, it could have been another Carrington Event. This was happening at the same time as the London Olympics and the appropriate members of the scientific and political world were anxious and alert (not that any of them could have done anything about it). It had significant effects on earth and still does. The hurricanes, global warming, mental health, and animal navigational confusion are all affected by solar magnetically shifting activity.

The reduction of the earth's magnetism, together with solar activity causing mental activity, results in an experience of agitation and inner turbulence, both globally and personally. The current age is defined as one of anxiety, insecurity, instability, both within and without – the individual and the world. They are the same; one reflects the other.

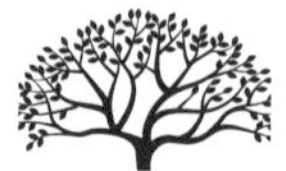

The psychopathology in the socio-political world is a manifestation of the personal mental meltdown. The insanity of 2016 is still referred to and contemplated with disbelief using every psychological term available for insanity. And it is a further example of repetition. Approximately a hundred years ago the psychosocial climate in Europe was almost the same. It was the age of Expressionism, which represented angst, isolation, fear, and a sense of impending doom, itself fulfilled by World War I. Now the impending doom (or at least the worst of it) is nuclear war on the physical plane and personal annihilation on the psychological one. The aftermath of WWII resulted in the Cold War of the early '60s which was also a time of enormous psychosocial and political anxiety – cultural revolution, actual revolution, and a threat of nuclear annihilation far greater than the one we face today.

This age of anxiety is not a new phenomenon, but a very old one that is repeating itself after a century of unprecedented progress in all areas of human endeavour and discovery.

The other life-altering, enthralling and eagerly anticipated event of 2012 was the announcement from Cern, Switzerland, of the identification of the Higgs Boson. Young physicists from all over the world camped out in order to be present for the announcement on July 4th that the missing particle had been found. It was referred to as the 'god particle' and turned out to be not a particle at all, but a field. Sean Carroll describes this label as great marketing, because it excites so much more interest than 'we've finally discovered a field'. This is not the space to describe the road to the discovery of the Higgs. For that, I suggest Sean Carroll's fascinating, entertaining, and highly informative book, *The Particle at the End of the Universe.*

It's an amusing challenge to write a book of this sort and deliberately avoid the word 'god'. Our instinctual need to anthropomorphise intangible things (actually, tangible items also) has caused insanity, conflict and gender war.

My intention is to demonstrate the links between science, alchemy, quantum mechanics, quantum fields, superstring theory, and the wisdom that manifests repeatedly over the centuries with consciousness: Avery Hopkins, Dennis W Hauck, Charles Haanal, Neville Goddard, Alice Bailey, Raja Choudhury, Andrew Holecek, Sam Harris, Alan B. Wallace – all describing the one thinking substance that fills all space, from and through which all things are made. All of these neuroscientists, spiritual philosophers, alchemists and Buddhists are in agreement about the one reality: consciousness.

In Raja Choudhury's lecture 'Hacking Your Consciousness Indian Style' he explores the possibilities of altering consciousness by reprogramming the brain. This is what he means by hacking and he approaches it from several angles – base instinct, physical requirements (diet etc.,) and methods for altering the brain both chemically and naturally. (He was the source for the information on LSD in chapter 1.) He explains the four levels of consciousness and the potential power of meditation to experience the fourth state which is the Unified Field of stillness, transcendence and silence. At the outset of this talk he announces the complete absence of spirituality and religion in consideration of the subject and takes a wholly scientific approach throughout. This is highly unusual because he is so renowned for his authority and insight into Kundalini, Tantra, Shiva/Shakti and all Indian philosophy and is always inspirational. He never reads (his lectures), but exudes enthusiasm and conviction.

John Hagelin is a neuroscientist and astrophysicist who also gave a lecture at Stanford University entitled 'Hacking Human Consciousness', Stanford being one of the main research bases for this study. He lectures globally on superstring theory, consciousness, the secret behind 'The Secret' (the best-selling book by Rhonda Byrne published in 2004), quantum fields, Higgs Boson, astronomy, politics – there isn't much he doesn't know and think about. He delivers absorbing lectures on the benefits of meditation and the powers of transcendence. The following is a paraphrase of one given on the 8th September 2014:

> 'With the discovery of the unified field, the so-called superstring field, we now know that all life in all of its diversity is, basically, one. And, that unity of mind and matter is consciousness – universal consciousness. There is a single

> field of intelligence which unites gravity with electromagnetism, light with radioactivity and the nuclear force, so that all the forces of nature combine. The unified field is a non-material field – it is the field of consciousness. We are all – people, animals, plants, planets, everything – all waves of vibration of this underlying superstring field. Knowing this through experience is called enlightenment.
>
> 'In quantum mechanics, the idea of particle is replaced by the idea of wave function (field). The field that is waving is made of the same stuff as thought. It is a universal ocean of pure abstract potential existence; pure abstract self-aware consciousness which rises in waves of vibration to create – everything.
>
> 'It is experienced in diversity because we are all different vibrational frequencies – natural frequencies within the field. Our whole universe is a symphony of varying harmonics and overtones.'

He goes on to describe the unified field as being self-aware and dynamically interacting with and responding to its own presence. This is how the non-material field of intelligence sequentially manifests the multiplicity of the universe. The human mind is able to access this unified field through transcendence which is achieved in meditation. There are different levels of thought just as there are of the physical world's scale of reality which moves from superficial, distracted 'busy' thinking – preoccupied with the next event and one's to-do list, to that of greater concentration when learning and absorbing information. Then there is a deeper level which is one of intense creativity and *flow* when one feels part of a greater life force. There is the quantum level of theory, mechanics, and physics and the ultimate silence of the unified field – the USM – which is transcendence, enlightenment, and the source of manifestation. It could be illustrated like this:

Meditation + Intention = Physical Reality

Unified Field + Intention = Dynamic Field

The purpose in juxtaposing Raja Choudhury and John Hagelin is to demonstrate the unified thinking between two men from entirely different cultures and continents who pursue contrasting passions and careers (art, philosophy and spirituality; astrophysics, neuroscience and astronomy) and who adopt very different styles of delivery and communication. And they both elevate meditation as the single most effective method for transformation and change. The world within and above becomes the world without and below.

Sam Harris also promotes meditation for the many benefits that it affords, not least that of manifestation:

> 'Whatever the ultimate relationship between consciousness and matter, almost everyone will agree that at some point in the development of complex organisms like ourselves, consciousness seems to emerge ... the birth of consciousness must be the result of organisation: arranging atoms in certain ways appears to bring about an experience of being that very collection of atoms. This is undoubtedly one of the deepest mysteries given to us to contemplate.'
>
> — Sam Harris, *Waking Up*

Sixty-five years earlier, Neville Goddard said:

> 'Imagining oneself into the feeling of the wish fulfilled is the means by which a new state is entered. This gives the quality of is-ness. **Hermes** tells us: "That which is, is manifested; that which has been or shall be, is unmanifested, but not dead; for Soul, the eternal activity of God, animates all things".'

Here, from one who does not use the word 'god' in any meaningful way, is a suggested translation:

> The unified field revealed by the Higgs Boson and superstring theory is the thinking substance that fills all space, from and through which all things are made. I am that; I am that substance (that I will not call god) and therefore, I am the creator of my reality, experience and world. In chapter IV we observed that the conscious awareness of the artist impacts the art which, inevitably, impacts the audience, **and** that the audience also contributes to this process so that at the unified level of dynamically interacting intelligence, the level of transcendence which can be reached through the practice of meditation, the triune elements that constitute 'a performance' become one – *the one thing* –

The Philosopher's Stone of performance. In this field of Being anxiety is not possible, poor confidence is utterly meaningless and fear cannot exist.

VIII. Silence

'Silence is not the absence of sound, but the presence of an inward listening awareness, an attunement of the mind's ear and an orientation of the spirit towards a certain inner stillness – perhaps the positive counterpoint to loneliness which so often thrives amid the crowd.'

— Pablo Neruda – *Ode to Silence*

'Silence remains, inescapably, a form of speech.... it has its own aesthetic, and learning to wield it is among the great arts of living.'

— Susan Sontag

We know that actual silence is not possible and in that regard does not exist. There is no need to identify, prove or explain that here because it is of no relevance. What is relevant is the silence that can be initiated anywhere and at any time irrespective of external cacophony. At the conclusion of his lectures or at the start of a meditation (which could be the same moment), Neville Goddard would say 'And now let us go into the silence.' This is the chosen, personal, deliberate and conscious silence of our 'world within'. It is the absence of distraction and an internal quietness that is not invaded by external events.

Silence can make us feel very uncomfortable. The pianist John Ogden described its power when performing Liszt's B Minor Sonata. If he was brave enough to sit in silence at the piano for twenty seconds before starting to play, the tension in the audience was so electric that their contribution and involvement from the start was visceral and intense. And how fascinating the use of the word brave. Most, if not all, performers consider bravery necessary in order to produce the required sounds and noises, not in doing nothing and being still. But, of course, it is not nothing; it is performing at a profound and meaningful level, and to sustain the tension that silence can create is brave indeed and is challenge enough for non-musicians. Gaps in the flow of conversation are usually avoided and utter nonsense can pour forth as a result. There is anxiety over having enough to talk about in certain situations – visiting a hospital patient or meeting someone new.

In everyday parlance, objects and decor are described as talking points thereby fulfilling a need to maintain the constant hum of the human voice.

Silence can be experienced as threatening, even in subtle, highly acceptable and mostly unnoticed circumstances such as the automaticity of putting music on, or the news, which isn't news but an addiction to a lust for events and an aversion to quietness. What then is the threat? Being alone without distraction has become a pervasive source of anxiety and one that is all too easily avoided. This is why fear intensifies in the early hours of the morning, but even then one can reach for the phone which can instantly alleviate a sense of isolation and begin its magic of distraction in a whole variety of ways.

Some years ago I interviewed a senior maths teacher about the amount of distraction pupils subjected themselves to while supposedly doing homework. He told me that the difficulty arose in exams because of the silence; they find the quietness to be the invasive force that undermines their concentration – they simply are not used to it.

Paul Goodman, the great twentieth century novelist, poet, playwright and psychotherapist, identified the nine kinds of silence present in life in his exemplary book *Speaking and Language* (Public Library 1972):

> 'Not speaking and speaking are both human ways of being in the world and there are kinds and grades of each. There is the dumb silence of slumber or apathy; the sober silence that goes with a solemn animal face; the fertile silence of awareness, pasturing the soul, whence emerge new thoughts; the alive silence of alert perception, ready to say, "This... this... "; the musical silence that accompanies absorbed activity; the silence of listening to another speak, catching the drift and helping him be clear; the noisy silence of resentment and self-recrimination, loud but subvocal speech, but sullen to say it; baffled silence; the silence of peaceful accord with other persons or communion with the cosmos.'

John Cage (1912 – 1992) was a composer, philosopher, writer, and Buddhist. In 1968 a collection of his writings and lectures were published and collectively entitled 'Silence.' Cage was highly influenced by the Zen philosophy of nothing – no thing, and the concept of silence.

> 'You could conclude an evolution... from my works. The early ones could have been considered expressive. It sometimes seemed to me that I managed to "say" something in them. When I discovered India, what I was saying started to change. And when I discovered China and Japan, I changed the very fact of saying anything: I said nothing anymore. Silence: since everything already communicates, why wish to communicate? ... The silences speak for me, they demonstrate quite well that I am no longer there.'

Cage spent years searching for the perfect silence, believing that it was equivalent to God. He inserted deliberate silences into his works both written and musical. In 1952 at Harvard University he experienced an anechoic chamber and genuinely hoped to find the silence he thought would enlighten him. He wanted to find and confront the nothing.

> 'In this moment of voidness, Cage's ears fill up with sound. He is stunned! It is not what he'd been expecting! Where's the silence!?! He's hearing a dull roar and a high whine! He rushes from the anechoic chamber and urges

the engineer to explain.... The high whine ... is the firing of his neurons. The dull roar is the blood flowing through Cage's veins.'

— Kay Larson, *Where the Heart Beats* (2012) Penguin.

'And it appeared to me, when I went through my work, or what was to become my work, that the experience that I had had in the soundproof room at Harvard was a turning point. I had honestly and naively thought that some actual silence existed. So I had not really thought about the question of silence. I had not really put silence to the test. I had never looked into its impossibility. So when I went into that sound-proof room I really expected to hear nothing. With no idea of what nothing could sound like. The instant I heard myself produce two sounds [...] I was stupefied. For me, that was the turning point. In other words, there is no split between spirit and matter. And to realise this we have only suddenly to awake to the fact.'

— John Cage from *Where the Heart Beats* – Larson.

The fact that Cage awoke to was that of non-duality, of the essence of being which is ceaseless and noisy. Absolute silence is physically fictional and this, for Cage, was mind-changing and therefore life-altering; this experience was the source of 4'33". What is fascinating is Cage's absorption in Zen Buddhism and his (self-confessed) naivety regarding the scientific reality of silence. It seems paradoxical that one so immersed in conceptual art and life could overlook the conceptual nature of silence. But that's the difference sixty years can make, and has.

The silence that Cage sought caused his anxiety by its absence. We cannot know what response he may have had to its presence if such a possibility had been able to occur. The acquisition of the many scientific breakthroughs – cosmic exploration, quantum mechanics, string theory, the Higgs Boson and dark matter – has not served to reduce anxiety levels which have, as we have noted, increased considerably. Technological progress always contains duality in terms of human benefit. That is because of the global (dis)organisation of every kind of resource. Our expanded understanding of every facet of scientific theory and practice and of how the universe operates is paralleled with the ever increasing speed and immediacy of distraction, diversion and noise. And never have we felt so busy, so overloaded and short of time – and so anxious.

When we get up to perform, the inner silence that is mostly ignored confronts us, however briefly. For many people this silence is the cause of anxiety because it isn't recognised; so little time and attention has been spent there. Just like the maths pupils struggling in their exams with unfamiliar mental territory, we can feel like visitors abroad in a landscape that we'd rather not be in. It can be compared to 'dark matter' in that its unknown components can be frightening for that very reason – we don't know what they are, i.e. who we are. This is the cause of anxiety, and the cure is to explore and discover the world within, know our way around it so that it is familiar, secure, peaceful and quiet. It feels like a home you want to live in; it feels invincible – and it is. When John Ogden sat in silence for an unusually long time before starting the B Minor Sonata, he caused the entire audience to briefly confront their own inner landscapes and to share the silence and the tension so that when he began to play, the performance was shared as a powerful, dynamic and profound experience.

> 'Our deepest feelings are precisely those we are least able to express, and even in the act of adoration, silence is our highest praise.'
>
> — Neville Goddard

In chapter V reference was made to the *Quintessence.* In alchemy this is the fifth element which is not really an element at all. It is the product or result of the four elements in union.

> 'The Quintessence is a thing that is spiritual, penetrating, tingeing and incorruptible, which emerges anew from the Four Elements when they are bound together.'
>
> — Isaac Newton

Every practice identifies the Quintessence. Hindu alchemy defines it as *prana* which is breath; in tantric alchemy it is *kundalini* (chapter IV); in Taoist alchemy it is *chi (*energy) and in Chinese alchemy it is *growth.* In each instance it is the *energetic life force* which can be harnessed and made use of, or ignored and be controlled by. Consider our use of the word quintessential; we use it to describe that which we perceive as definitive, ultimate, pure and unsurpassable. And that's what it is; essentially invisible, but potentially everywhere. It is the transcendence in meditation, the risen kundalini, the liberation of impermanence and the eternal absence of anxiety in all its forms. Quintessence is the alchemy of silence.

Early alchemists were both physicists and psychologists and operated within two laboratories – one within, the other without. They were mystics and meditated committedly as part of their inner and outer practice. Every aspect of their activity, including thought and awareness, corresponded scientifically, spiritually and psychologically. This was (and is) true holisticism. This inner laboratory was 'a quiet place the alchemist created within himself, a place of no confusion where the Work could proceed on his soul'. (Dennis Hauck – *The Emerald Tablet.*)

The Gift of Silence is the title of a TedX talk given by Nick Seaver in 2015. He and his wife embarked on an eighteen month Shamatha Project organised by Alan B. Wallace and Clifford Saron which was the first long-term scientific investigation into the effects of sustained silence and meditation. Before they left their busy corporate New York lifestyle in 2007 he amusingly describes his mind as being like a bad neighbourhood – somewhere you don't want to go to alone. It took eighteen months to validate and ensure the scientific findings, i.e. the multiple benefits arising from meditation practice (all of which are exhaustively documented as footnotes). In order for anyone to enjoy these benefits we need to practise the exploration of our potentially silent inner world for a mere ten minutes a day. No fee, no travel, no equipment – and the beginning of the end of anxiety, doubt and loss.

At the beginning of this book the subject was play, which inevitably led to a focus on children and childhood. In subsequent chapters we have noted how the natural aptitude that preschool children usually possess can gradually become eroded through adult attitudes, expectations, and constraints. This aptitude is physical, psychological, spiritual and emotional and it affects, therefore, all aspects of experience. Small children have an extraordinary capacity for silence, peace and quietness, just as they do for poise, concentration and imaginative play. They don't separate work from creation and attention because it is meaningless to them. As adults we do precisely that and as a consequence need to undergo a process (or several) of what is, essentially, recognition; we already know what we think we are learning. Most of the information we absorb most readily is due to re-cognition – knowing it again – and many of the teachers that we consider exceptional are those that we agree with.

The ability to discover that which we know and possess is achieved through repeated exploration of our world within in the relative 'silence' of meditation. We don't actually forget anything; our recall may suffer miserably, but our memory is intact. In meditation we remove obstacles to reveal what has always been there. Transformation for artists is an alchemical process because it involves the necessary inner application to reveal the desired *and known* liberated creativity which everybody feels somewhere within. The fertile solitude of creation is one of the many gifts of silence, and children have a natural capacity for it – which means that we all do.

(fn The Shamatha Project was the most comprehensive and exhaustive study of meditation to (that) date. During the retreat the neuro-scientific effects of prolonged meditation were measured and studied partly in order to provide the practice of meditation and its many benefits with conclusive scientific evidence that could assist in the growth and development of all humanity. (fn TedX YouTube). It was

an enormous undertaking both to organise and endure, but not one participant experienced anything less than a total shift in perception, attitude and well-being. Saronlab.ucdavis.edu/shamathaproject)

Chapter Summaries

Part I

Chapter I – Play and Practice

Examining the perception of both, separately and together, and the habitual psychological approaches that define our experience. Defining and thereby liberating these concepts to reveal the relationship between the two.

Chapter II – Attitude and Motivation

An exploration of intrinsic motivation in vocational disciplines such as music and an enquiry into how and why it often diminishes, irrespective of ability and achievement. The need for approval, support and encouragement to maintain motivation and the power of peer influence in adolescence to affect attitude and self-esteem.

Chapter III – Emotion and Imagination

The impact of the imagination and learning to use it to gain control over powerful reactive emotions, when either desired or necessary. Guidance to the difference between emotion and feeling, and the ways in which we are always interacting with, and in, the vibrational world. An explanation of morphic resonance and of visualisation techniques and applications.

Chapter IV – Anxiety and Mind

Investigating the source of fear, the cause of stress and the misconception of self.

The misuse of imagination and the dependency on approval and praise for personal validation. The 'fraud syndrome' and the power of social veneer. Meditation.

Part 2

Chapter V – Background and Introduction to Alchemy

Surveying the roots of alchemy in ancient Egypt and its core structure of the triune principle, which illuminates the meaning of 'As above, so below, as within, so without'. Identifying Hermes Trismegistus, Thoth, Paracelsus, the Emerald Tablet and the Philosopher's Stone. Illustrating the correspondences between alchemy and Kundalini practices and the links that so many esoteric disciplines share in the quest for 'The One Thing', of which we are all a part and wish to experience. The use of symbolism and art and the absence of religion.

Chapter VI – The Alchemy of Performance

The alchemical process and its practical application in daily life. The two laboratories – inner and outer with our focus on the inner. The three phases: Negredo, Albedo and Rubedo, the eight stages within them. How to understand, internalise and apply the practice to achieve lasting liberation from inhibiting anxiety, underachievement and personal suffering.

Chapter VII – The Wisdom of Repetition

The heart of this chapter is about the cyclic nature of everything – above and below, within and without; the microcosm and the macrocosm. Its aim is to identify and illustrate the plethora of connections between seemingly disparate strata of existence and to demonstrate the *inevitability* of how and why we all not only fit in, but are indispensable to the whole. Repetition is the key. It can be destructive or its truth marvelled at – it depends on one's perception and **consciousness.**

Chapter VIII – Silence

This chapter links with chapter IV in that it leads us into the realms of silence (or just quietness and being alone) and is designed to be something of a hand-holding wander through the meaning and deliverance of quietness and the world within which can feel threatening if experienced as foreign territory. It is to promote hope, courage and curiosity to explore the redemptive power of meditation and solitude in any of their guises.

Appendix 1

Alchemy and Buddhism

Nichiren Buddhism recognises that all of life is deeply connected and that it is impossible to be truly happy in isolation. It encourages practising for others as well as ourselves and its principle aim is known as Kosen-Rufu which means world peace and the action to realise it. It involves chanting, which is an outward projection of one's sound, to connect with the rest of humanity as well as with the vibrational world. It is a sharing activity and can be focused on specific intentions, but always involves unity and inclusion. It is a totally human spiritual practice. The nine levels of consciousness correspond with those of quantum scientific fields as identified by physicists and neuro-scientists. The first five levels are the physical senses and the remaining four are desires, conscious mind, subconscious mind and USM (transcendence). This current age of conflict, anxiety, and alienation was predicted and identified as one that Nichiren

Buddhism was designed to address. It is not esoteric, impenetrable or foreign. It is for all humanity and recognises the Buddha nature in everyone. The practice is to remove the obstacles that conceal it and to assist others to do the same.

On February 9th 2017 at the Nourse Theatre San Francisco, CA, Alan Wallace, a world renowned author and Buddhist scholar trained by the Dalai Lama, and Sean Carroll, a world renowned theoretical physicist and best-selling author, discussed 'The Nature of Reality' from spiritual and scientific viewpoints. Their dialogue was mediated by theoretical physicist and author Marcelo Gleiser, director of Dartmouth Institute for Cross-Disciplinary Engagement. The following is a paraphrase of Alan Wallace's summary:

> Our scientific way of addressing the mind is not scientific; we are not rigorously observing the phenomenon we are trying to understand. Introspection plays no role in the modern scientific study of the mind. Buddhism is not a religion. It is a radically empirical way of investigating the nature of reality from the inside out; an investigation of the mind from inside itself – an open mind to be observed

as it flows with a truly objective and factual investigation of its functions.

Alchemy and Buddhism are both about transformation – as within so without, as above so below. They both recognise that one's level of consciousness is the source of cause and effect which creates our world. They are not religions. Those who might be concerned about the absence of god need not worry. It is as if you are leaning against St. Paul's Cathedral while studying a map trying to locate it; it's far too close to identify. It is you.

Appendix 2

Meditation Techniques

This is a guide for those who don't currently have a meditation practice and who might find the navigation of available choices both on and offline daunting. For a beginner it's advisable to start with short guided sessions (10 – 15 minutes maximum) in order to build something sustainable.

The variety is no bad thing; one has to survey the field and 'shop around' to some extent to discover what suits. The focus is not to lose sight of the motive for the search in the first place. Our needs shift and change and there are multiple meditation techniques able to accommodate them. But, as we develop and explore the practice, what becomes increasingly apparent is the common denominator shared by them all, which is the quest for having the capacity to dwell quietly and peacefully in our inner landscape, to become familiar and at ease with it and to create an internal haven that our minds want to be in. It is liberating, constantly available and free. No equipment is necessary and there's nothing to be a member of. If membership, group commitment and wearing special robes are appealing, there is no shortage of outlets. Organisations are happy to take three figure sums to give you a mantra (meaningless word) to repeat on four consecutive days in order for you to experience transcendence, but there is no guarantee that you will, nor are there refunds.

We are so fortunate to have the internet, which is replete with guidance for just about everything including meditation. Some of it is extremely beneficial; most of it is not. My intention here is to provide a succinct guide to help you to navigate the plethora of tempting offers promising enlightenment in a week, or cures for all troubles be they physical, personal or financial. YouTube works through networking which means that when you find something that resonates well with you, it will lead you along an appropriate path. But, be selective even then. Here follows a list with links of a few of the most accessible, insightful and immediately beneficial online guided meditations for beginners or 'sporadic' meditators.

Sam Harris – Mindfulness Guided Meditation (short version 9 minutes; long version – with music 30 minutes).

Eckhart Tolle – Stillness Meditation – 11.23 minutes; Guided Meditation (onion layers) 12.41 minutes.

How to Manifest Anything – YouArecreators.org. – 11.42 minutes.

Kelly Howell – Universal Mind Meditation I and II. Brainsync.com This lasts for 35 minutes, but is designed to be listened to while falling asleep.

Dauschey – Become Limitless. This also works subliminally so the length is irrelevant as you will soon be unconscious. It's a different approach to meditation and can be used in conjunction with other alert practices during which you sit and remain conscious.

There are many more – these suggestions are simply designed to help launch you on your own personal path of exploration of the world within.

Here is a ten minute mindfulness meditation to try:

Sit comfortably in a chair or on the floor if you prefer, but be sure that you're not preoccupied with physical challenges arising from awkward positions.

Take around five conscious deeper-than-usual breaths allowing the air to 'fall' into your abdomen. As you do this, notice a subtle draft at the tip of the nostrils as you inhale.

Let your eyes close, keeping the focus on the breath just as it is now – no need for deliberately deeper inhalations. Make an inner secret smile and feel its effect.

Now we're going to move the focus around just a little. Notice your 'inner hands' – the vibrational field of your hands. It might feel like mild pins and needles and you will have no sensation of your outer hands which could be any shape or not be there at all.

Stay with this feeling which is quite pleasant. Let your breathing be as it is, maybe noticing the slight draft as you inhale every now and then.

Thoughts will be flying around, but take no special interest. They can be like small children playing in the distance – possibly a nuisance, but too far away to matter. As with any noises that may arise, simply notice without reaction.

Nearly done.... tingling inner hands, nostril draft and, lastly, focus on the point between your eyebrows. You may even experience a definite sensation of pressure there. Maintain these focal points in an alert yet effortless way for ten breaths which you count on the in breath.

Take a deeper breath now and gently clench your fists two or three times. Now an even deeper breath and slowly count from five to one, rising upwards, at which point allow your eyes to open and take in your surroundings.

Try not to rush off and when and wherever you do go, take some of this with you.

Appendix 3

Alchemy and Addiction

Compulsive behaviour very often starts in childhood and depending on its severity is treated with medication or some form of psychotherapy, or is simply tolerated or ignored completely. It is in adolescence that the increasing availability of escape mechanisms in the form of substances and of behaviour can result in habitual relief from unpleasant and perhaps disturbing psychological states. Even without a background of childhood emotional disorder, the degree of pressure and stress that teenagers are exposed to is frequently intolerable (to them) and strategies have to be sought in order to endure daily experience. ('Teenagers' may be getting younger, but they are also growing older; adulthood no longer carries the same authority in terms of the number of years spent on the planet.)

Dependency on something external to oneself is not unusual and the perception of addiction can be quite personal; it depends on the level of desire to behave otherwise and the degree of mental preoccupation absorbed in the object of compulsion. Also, there is mental and physical addiction, and the former is probably more problematic because it is governed by emotion which dominates thought every time. The cycle is well documented; the ensuing self-loathing perpetuates the need for relief – and all addiction is a source of relief.

Adolescents love rewards and prizes – personal prizes such as peer approval, recognition, excitement through new experience and being seen to survive it all with ease. A substance that provides immediate relief is also a huge reward, but so is surrendering to a compulsion to clean your teeth eight times before leaving the house – it is still a relief, because of the effort involved in trying to resist it. The word addiction is used so liberally that its true definition is always debatable. As suggested earlier, there is no single definition because it is as much a psychological experience as a clinical diagnosis. Most people feel that there are aspects of their appetites and needs that would benefit from greater control and it is exactly this degree of control that best defines addiction.

Addicts seek to alter the way they feel; that's usually how it all starts. Many people enjoy drinking, taking recreational drugs and eating delicious food because it can be extremely enjoyable. The tipping point is when the excess becomes a need and the enjoyment mostly evaporates; the notion of free will is then very remote and this is where addiction is mostly misunderstood. Addicts are often searching for something that feels elusive or even impossible and have a powerful urge to escape from the void that is left. Fear is the principle cause and, as we have seen, fear is illusory, which isn't particularly consoling for a frightened person. The application of the internal alchemical processes explained in chapter VI can transform addiction into release, into liberation. Addicts are in search of an altered state and are often very spiritually oriented. In the case of alcohol the process of its production has a parallel with the psychological process of relieving our dependency on it. It is spirit; we are spirit. Calcination, dissolution, separation, conjunction, fermentation, distillation and coagulation are the means by which we can transform ourselves and discover that that which we have been seeking in the world without has been residing in our world within all along. The alchemical process is able to systematically remove the obstacles to reveal its presence.

Appendix 4

The Wisdom of Brevity

Alchemy is the process of revealing the true essence of something whether it be a metal, a plant or a personality. It systematically removes the ephemera to find the source that truly matters in terms of absorption to produce growth – of substance, consciousness, life. In the face of so much criticism regarding concentration levels and attention spans, it must be conceded that brain efficiency is potentially much improved as a result of our knowledge of its function. No one can convincingly argue that thirty years ago time was better spent waiting for public transport to travel to a library in order to access books that couldn't be borrowed and to spend the hours taking notes in longhand and to return daily for as long as necessary. Information was absorbed in a very different way then, partly because of the value placed on its availability. That value has altered radically and with it our attitude towards learning.

We have seen how mind maps exploit the brain's absorption efficiency by using images that reflect radiant thinking thereby minimising time spent on committing information to long term memory. It's true that we absorb that which is relevant at any particular time, but that time isn't fixed. The brain stores, files, and cross references swathes of information that it makes use of months and years later. The instant access to information has changed the *way* in which we absorb it, which isn't necessarily a loss to the nation's intellectual stature, but it's a struggle to adapt the methods of education in order to accommodate the fiercely rapid technological growth. The way we educate children is archaic and at least two hundred years out of date.

Zen Buddhism is known for its brevity and simplicity. One doesn't have to spend years in earnest study memorising and chanting the lengthy Sutras, and many of the lessons consist of short, pithy and subtly amusing insights. (Read Alan Watts for copious examples). In Nicherin Buddhism the daily chanting of the Lotus Sutra was drastically shortened fifteen years ago because it was considered to be far too long for today's lifestyle and was reduced to its *essence* which now takes about eight minutes as opposed to forty. It can be likened to Haiku poetry and art – profoundly and beautifully distilled. So often in life, less is more.

Appendix 5

Daily Alignments

Here is a list of short and simple tasks that are easily included as and when they suit you throughout the day. They are not to be obsessed about or stressed over and they don't all need to be done every day. They are to be used rather than obeyed and adapted to the variable nature of daily life. It is a guide to get you started whenever the need arises and, even if used sporadically at first, some benefit will be felt and with it the knowledge that it is there to be resumed at any time. After the list there is an explanation of each item with links where applicable.

Read your Gratitude Book

Do three minutes Pranyama breathing

Practise Brain Yoga sequence (four/five minutes)

Meditate

Study for fifteen/twenty minutes

Spend time outdoors with some form of nature

Write your Gratitude Book

A gratitude book is a notebook in which you write at least ten things that you are thankful for that day. Even on a bad day there are plenty of things to appreciate and if you feel really stuck remember the basics – the ability to see, walk, sleep indoors, and even to write. You will soon find it difficult to keep to ten items, and of course you don't have to! Write in the evening and read it in the morning.

Pranyama breathing is a yoga practice known also as alternate nostril breathing. It enhances your feeling of well being and of focus. A clear demonstration of the technique can be found here:

https://www.youtube.com/watch?v=395ZloN4Rr8

Brain Yoga is a technique for aligning and balancing the two hemispheres of the brain. It's pleasant to do and a good example to follow is Janine's which is here:

> https://www.youtube.com/watch?v=d8uDl0_T5QI&t=136s

Meditate – see appendix 2.

Studying isn't any heavy duty research. It is simply forming the habit of connecting_with insightful guidance on any of the subject areas covered in this book – and_beyond. It can take the form of reading, watching a YouTube video, listening to a short talk (or part of a long one) and even a discussion with someone.

Spending time outdoors may be something most of us do anyway, but the inclusion here is so as to raise our awareness of what is out there, all of which_we are a_part, and to_*feel* that connection. Notice the vegetation and life forms around you. There are more trees, plants and birds in any city than we tend to realise, and which we mostly ignore. It is all about observation – without and within.

References

Chapter I – Play and Practice

Ian Bogost *Play Anything – The pleasure of limits, the uses of boredom, & the secret of games* (Basic Books 2016)

John Sloboda *Exploring the Musical Mind – cognition, emotion, ability, function* (OUP 2005)

John Sloboda *et al. The Leverhulme Project 1994 – 1996*

Alison Gopnik *The Philosophical Baby* (Bodley Head 2009)

—— *The Gardener and the Carpenter* (Bodley Head 2016)

Chapter II – Attitude and Motivation

Carl Jung *Psychology and Alchemy* (First published in England by Routledge 1953. Second edition completely revised 1968. Reprinted 2010)

Alice Bailey *The Consciousness of the Atom* (Published by Start Publishing LLC 2012 from a series of eight lectures delivered in New York winter 1921/22)

Andrew Evans *Performing Confidence* (A&C Black, London 2003)

Lehmann, Sloboda and Woody *Psychology for Musicians* (OUP 2007)

Neville Goddard *The Power of Awareness* (Sublime Books 2016)

Chapter III – Emotion and Imagination

Michael Bradford *Consciousness: The New Paradigm* (The Institute for Consciousness Research 2017)

U.S. Anderson *Three Magic Words* (Stellar Books 2014)

—— *The Magic in Your Mind* (Stellar Editions 2016. First published 1961)

Rollin McCraty *http://:www.heartmath.org*

Rupert Sheldrake *The Science Delusion* (Coronet 2012)

——http://www.sheldrake.org/research/morphic

Shakti Gawain *Creative Visualisation; Living in the Light; Developing Intuition – The Shakti Gawain Essentials* (Mango Media Inc. 2015)

B. Alan Wallace and Brian Hodel *Embracing Mind – the common ground between science and spirituality* (Shambhala Publications Inc 2008)

Judith Becker *Deep Listeners* (Indiana University Press 2004)

Chapter IV – Anxiety and Mind

Raja Choudhury *Hacking Your Consciousness – Indian Style* (Lecture delivered at the International Indian Centre, New Delhi on 14th September 2016)

Alice Bailey *The Consciousness of the Atom* (Start Publishing LLC 2012)

Eckhart Tolle *The Power of Now and Practicing the Power of Now* (New World Library Novato, California www.newworldlibrary.com)

——*A New Earth* (Penguin Books 2005)

Oliver Sachs *Musicophilia* (first published 2008 by Vintage Books, a division of Random House, Inc., NY)

—— *Gratitude* (First published in UK 2015 by Picador)

Sam Harris *Waking Up* (First published in UK 2014 by Bantam Press of Transworld Publishers)

—— *Free Will* (Free Press, Simon and Schuster,Inc 2012)

Julian Baggini *Freedom Regained – The Possibility of Free Will* (Granta Publications 2015)

—— *A Course in Miracles* (First published by the Foundation for Inner Peace USA 1975. Published in Great Britain by Arkana 1985)

Alan Watts *Does It Matter?* (First published by Pantheon Books 1970; Vintage Books 1971)

The Wisdom of Insecurity – A Message for an Age of Anxiety (Rider of Random Century Group first published 1954; UK 1974; reprinted 1987, 1989)

Daniel Goleman *Meditative Mind* (3rd Edition published by Thorsons 1996)

Chapter V – An Introduction to Alchemy

Avery Hopkins – Kymia Arts *An Introduction to Alchemy* (YouTube published September 20th 2016)

Dennis William Hauck *Sorcerer's Stone – A Beginner's Guide to Alchemy* (Crucible Books 2015)

—— *The Emerald Tablet – Alchemy for Personal Transformation* (Penguin Compass 1999)

—— *The Complete Idiot's Guide to Alchemy* (Alpha Books 2008)

Luxor Media *Alchemy – Sacred Secrets Revealed* (Published by mattquatsi. December 2011 http://www.luxormedia.org.)

Gnostic Students *Alchemy 01 – The Elements in Spiritual Growth*

——*Alchemy 02 – Transmutation*

——*Alchemy 03 – The Laboratory of the Alchemist*

——*Alchemy 04 – Laboratory Work*

——*Alchemy 05 – The Secret of Azoth*

——*Alchemy 06 – Mercury, Hermes*

——(Published by Glorian Publishing 2016 collectively entitled *Alchemy Secrets of Spiritual Transformation* and delivered as lectures and also available as online transcriptions.

—— https://www.atlasobscura.com/articles/how-alchemy-has-been-depicted-in-art-through-the-ages

Chapter VI – The Alchemy of Performance

Dennis William Hauck *The Emerald Tablet – Alchemy for Personal Transformation* (Penguin Compass 1999)

—— *The Complete Idiot's Guide to Alchemy* (Alpha Books 2008)

—— *Sorcerer's Stone – A Beginner's Guide to Alchemy* (Crucible Books 2015)

Avery Hopkins – Kymia Arts *Operative Alchemy – Open lecture published on Yo*

Carl Jung *Psychology and Alchemy* (First published in England by Routledge 1953. Second edition completely revised 1968. Reprinted 2010)

Luxor media *Alchemy – Sacred Secrets Revealed* (Published by mattquatsi December 2011 http://www.luxormedia.org.)

Gnostic Students *Alchemy Secrets of Spiritual Transformation* (Glorian Publishing 2016)

Chapter VII – The Wisdom of Repetition

Jordan B. Peterson Maps of Meaning – The Architecture of Belief. (Routledge 1999)

Ajit Mookerjee *Kundalini – The Arousal of Inner Energy* (Thames and Hudson 1982/2005)

Neville Goddard *The Creative Use of Imagination* (A series of lectures transcribed by Margaret Ruth Broome 1989 G & J Publishing Co.)

—— *A Course in Miracles* (First published by the Foundation for Inner Peace USA 1975. Published in Great Britain by Arkana 1985)

Michael Dawson *Healing the Cause* (Findhorn Press 1995)

Uwe Albrecht *Yes/No* (Hay House November 2012)

Raja Choudhury Lectures delivered at the India International Centre:

—— *Soma: The Psychedelic Origins of Religious Experience.* August 23rd 2015

—— *Kundalini: Awakening the Shakti Within* 27th September 2015

—— *The Art and Science of Meditation* 1st November 2015

—— *The Third Eye* 30th April 2016

——*Shiva: The Dance of Consciousness* 8th July 2016

John Hagelin Lectures delivered at Stanford University, USA:

——*Hacking Consciousness* July 2014

——*Is Consciousness the Unified Field?* July 2014

—— *Consciousness: A Quantum Physics Perspective* July 2014

Sam Harris *Waking Up* (Transworld Publishers – Bantam Press 2014)

David Eagleman *The Brain – The Story of You* (Canongate 2015)

https://earthobservatory.nasa.gov/IOTD/view.php?id=84266

Jim Self *A Course in Mastering Alchemy* MasteringAlchemy.com

Swami Sivananda Radha *Kundalini Yoga for the West* (Published by Timeless Books 1978 and 1993)

Carlo Rovelli *Reality Is Not What It Seems* (Allen Lane/Penguin Random House 2014)

Chapter VIII – Silence

Pablo Neruda *Keeping Quiet* (Extravagaria – Farrar, Straus & Giroux 2001. First Published 1958)

Susan Sonntag *The Aesthetics of Silence – the first essay in her book Styles of Radical Will 1969* (Public Library)

Paul Goodman *Speaking and Language* (NY Random House 1971)

John Cage *Silence* (First published in UK in 1968 by Calder & Boyars Ltd)

Kay Larson *Where the Heart Beats* (Penguin Group 2013)

Dennis William Hauck *The Emerald Tablet* (Penguin Compass 1999)

Neville Goddard *The Power of Awareness* (First published 1952. Reissued by Sublime Books 2016)

Nick Seaver *The Gift of Silence* (TEDX 2015 – The Shamatha Project)

* *The Shamatha Project was the most comprehensive and exhaustive study of meditation to (that) date. During the retreat the neuro-scientific effects of prolonged meditation were measured and studied*

partly in order to provide the practice of meditation and its many benefits with conclusive scientific evidence that could assist in the growth and development of all humanity. (fn TedX YouTube). It was an enormous undertaking both to organise and endure, but not one participant experienced anything less than a total shift in perception, attitude and well-being. Saronlab.ucdavis.edu/shamathaproject.

B. Alan Wallace and Brian Hodel *Embracing Mind – The common ground of science and spirituality* (Shambhala Publications, Inc. 2008)

Additional Bibliography

Michael J. Gelb and Kelly Howell *Brain Power – Improve Your Mind as You Age* (New World Library 2012)

Malcolm Gladwell *Outliers – The Story of Success* (Little, Brown and Co., 2008)

——Blink – The Power of Thinking Without Thinking (Back Bay Books/Little, Brown & Co., 2005)

Eloise Ristad *A Soprano on Her Head* (Real People Press 1982)

Stephen Chun-Tao Cheng *The Tao of Voice – A New East-West Approach to Transforming the Singing and Speaking Voice* (Destiny Books 1991)

Michael McCallion *The Voice Book* (Faber & Faber 1988, 1989, 1998)

Tony Buzan *The MindMap Book – Radiant Thinking* (BBC Worldwide Ltd. 1993)

Mitch Horowitz *One Simple Idea* (Crown Publishers of Random House LLC 2014)

Robert Wright *Why Buddhism is True* (Simon and Schuster 2017)

References

Charles Haanal *The Master Key System* (Start Publishing LLC 2012)

Robert Collier *Secret of the Ages* (Sublime Books 2013)

Neville Goddard *Feeling is the Secret* (First published 1944. Reissued by Stellar Books 2014)

—— *Awakened Imagination* (First published 1954. Reissued by Martino Publishing 2010

Caroline Myss *Anatomy of the Spirit* (Bantam 1997)

Andreas C. Lehmann, John A. Sloboda, Robert H. Woody *Psychology for Musicians – Understanding and Acquiring the Skills* (Oxford University Press 2007)

John Rink (Editor) *Musical Performance – A Guide to Understanding* (Cambridge University Press 2002)